amazelab

# MAKE YOUR OWN
# RAINBOW

## A COLOURFUL APPROACH TO ALL THINGS STEAM

# LEONIE BRIGGS

Crown House Publishing Limited
www.crownhouse.co.uk

First published by
Crown House Publishing Limited
Crown Buildings, Bancyfelin, Carmarthen, Wales, SA33 5ND, UK
www.crownhouse.co.uk
and
Crown House Publishing Company LLC
PO Box 2223, Williston, VT 05495, USA
www.crownhousepublishing.com

EU GPSR Authorised Representative
Easy Access System Europe Oü, 16879218
Address: Mustamäe tee 50, 10621, Tallinn, Estonia
Contact Details: gpsr.requests@easproject.com, +358 40 500 3575

British Library Cataloguing-in-Publication Data

A catalogue entry for this book is available from the British Library.

Print ISBN 978-178583690-9
Mobi ISBN 978-178583694-7
ePub ISBN 978-178583695-4
ePDF ISBN 978-178583696-1
LCCN 2023935259

Typeset by Palimpsest Book Production Ltd, Falkirk, Stirlingshire

Printed in the UK by
Pureprint, Uckfield, East Sussex

# DEDICATION

This book is dedicated to Alexandra, Lucas and all the amazingly curious young people who will change the world for the betterment of us all.

# Acknowledgements

I'd like to thank:

David Briggs, my husband – the list of things to thank you for is endless – thank you for everything!

Alexandra and Lucas Briggs plus the whole and ever-expanding mini Amazelab crew who test every idea to make sure they are as effective as possible. They are: Alex, Lucas, Ava, Erin, Lenny, Elsie B, Elsie O, Emilia, Oscar, Willam, Tommy, Layla and Ada and their parents for encouraging and allowing them to be a part of this project.

My parents Glenys and Stephen Hedland

My parents in law Stephen and Julie Briggs

Wider family and friends:

- Jane Hewitt – without Jane this book would not exist!

- Richard Fenwick of Plantlet Culture for his contribution to one of the activities

- Dr Lizzie Burns for her contribution to one of the activities in this book

- Jorden Birch and Laura Watford of STEMunity

- All the fantastic and amazing clients of Amazelab

- The local school community especially Hoyland Common Primary School

- Everyone at Crown House Publishing.

# Contents

## THE ACTIVITIES

# Introduction

## Creativity

Henri Matisse is famously supposed to have said that creativity takes courage. Scientists, engineers and mathematicians - those working on technological advances - can be just as creative as artists. You will struggle to find great discoveries that do not involve great creativity. Creative thinking is a process applying knowledge, intuition and skill to making or discovering something new - much like a scientific experiment. At one time the 'ingredients' were just individual entities, then the next moment you have taken them and created something that was not there before.

STEAM (science, technology, engineering, arts, mathematics) education and learning can be quite daunting. Never fear as Amazelab is here to show you just how colourful and creative these subjects can be. Using the imagery, make up and colours of the rainbow as our inspiration, we will take on scientific investigations and STEAM projects that will spark imagination and learning, either at home or in the classroom. Throughout this book we'll take on tricky subjects in a colourful, fun and creative manner, with a real emphasis on memorable learning.

## Why a rainbow?

All of the activities in this book involve rainbows. Why? Because there is so much engaging science behind the colours and light. Rainbows capture children's imaginations and prove a useful hook into scientific investigation in the early years and beyond. Even as an adult, seeing a rainbow in the wild is an exciting and uplifting experience - and with a little know-how, you can create your own.

White light is made up of all the colours of the rainbow. The colour that you see is dependent upon the amount of light, and its colour, being reflected or absorbed by an object. Each colour that we are able to see with the human eye has a different wavelength and energy. Within the eye is the retina, which has two kinds of receptors - rods and cones - for perceiving light. Rods help us to see objects in dim lighting, and they respond to all wavelengths of the visible spectrum in low light. Cones are responsible for sending colour information to the brain, and they respond to specific wavelengths. There are three different types of cone receptors, which allow us to see coloured light. They are sometimes classified as red (L-cone), green (M-cone) and blue (S-cone), These aid us in distinguishing millions of colours. For us to see colours, there must be at least a small amount of light.

So, we've learnt that white light is a mixture of all the colours of the rainbow. What happens if we shine this white light through a glass prism? Well, the light slows down and bends, which in turn causes the colours to spread out into a spectrum. We call this the visible light spectrum, because it is made up of all the colours that we are able to see. In nature, a rainbow is formed when white light passes through rain droplets. As we know, the different colours contained in white light have different wavelengths, so when they are refracted through the droplets, the colours are separated.

Why not try it for yourself? You can create a rainbow by shining a light source - for example, a torch - through a prism or a glass of water. As we will see as we get stuck into the activities in this book, there are many other fun, creative and interesting ways to take inspiration from the colours of the rainbow.

## Health and safety

Before we begin, we'll just need to go over a few words of warning.

Some of these activities will get messy! You may want to complete them outdoors or, if you are indoors, to use a protective surface (e.g. a large tray or plastic sheet). Remember that some ingredients - for example, food colouring - may stain, so please wear suitable clothing and wear rubber gloves to protect your hands.

Beware of any allergies, intolerances or sensitivities to the ingredients used in the activities.

Care must be taken when using knives, scissors or boiling water. Adult intervention is advised.

Children must be under the constant supervision of an adult when completing the activities.

# THE ACTIVITIES

# Activity 1
# Exploding rainbows

**Chemical reactions**

## You will need

- 1 x jug
- 1 x teaspoon
- 1 x protective sheet
- 7 x small clear containers
- Food colouring (red, orange, yellow, green, blue, indigo, violet)
- Baking soda
- White vinegar

## The instructions

1. This activity is a bit messy, so work outside or use a protective sheet. Place your seven containers in a row, and add a teaspoon of baking soda to each container.

2. Add two drops of food colouring to each container – red food colouring to the first container, orange to the second, yellow to the third, green to the fourth, blue to the fifth, indigo to the sixth and violet to the seventh. (If you don't have all the rainbow colours, you can just use whichever colours you do have.)

3. Pour vinegar into each of the containers. Aim for twice as much vinegar as baking soda. The reaction will happen quickly, so be sure to step away, watch carefully and enjoy your exploding rainbow.

# The science

Baking soda and vinegar react chemically because one is a base and the other is an acid. Baking soda is a basic compound with the scientific name 'sodium bicarbonate'. Vinegar is a diluted solution containing acetic acid. When we see the two react, it is, in fact, two separate reactions. The first is the acid-base reaction. When vinegar and baking soda are first mixed together, hydrogen ions in the vinegar react with the sodium and the bicarbonate ions in the baking soda. The result is that two new chemicals are formed: carbonic acid and sodium acetate.

The second reaction is a decomposition reaction. Carbonic acid (formed as a result of the first reaction) immediately begins to decompose into water and carbon dioxide. This gas is the same as you would find in a carbonated drink. The carbon dioxide rises to the top of the mixture. This creates the bubbles and foam that you see when you mix baking soda and vinegar.

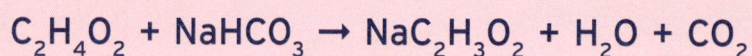

$$C_2H_4O_2 + NaHCO_3 \rightarrow NaC_2H_3O_2 + H_2O + CO_2$$

**vinegar + sodium bicarbonate → sodium acetate + water + carbon dioxide**

# Next level learning

How does the shape of the container influence the chemical reaction? If you mix a large amount of baking soda and vinegar in a small container with a narrow opening, expect an impressive explosion!

What ratios of vinegar to baking soda produce the largest volume of gas and the most impressive explosion? You could simply measure the height of the bubbles produced with a ruler.

Create different colour combinations to investigate primary and secondary colours.

Investigate rainbows in light and nature.

# Making curriculum links

| Early years foundation stage (EYFS) | Active learning, playing and exploring, thinking critically, creating with materials, experimenting with colour, explaining processes, fine motor skills, building relationships, managing self, speaking, listening, communication, attention and understanding. |
| --- | --- |
| Primary | Reading and following instructions, mathematics, working scientifically, materials, light, art and design. |
| Secondary | Working scientifically, particles, atoms, elements and compounds, chemical reactions, gas tests, pressure, colour, chemical changes and chemical analysis. |

# Activity 2
# Rainbow bridge

## Capillary action

**You will need**

- 7 x clear containers
- Paper towels
- Water
- Food colouring (red, yellow, blue)

## The instructions

1. Place your containers in a row. Add water to the first, third, fifth and seventh container.

2. To the first and the seventh container, add five drops of red food colouring. (You could use another colour if you don't have red, but you will need the colours specified to create a rainbow.) To the third container, add five drops of yellow food colouring. To the fifth container, add five drops of blue food colouring.

3. Make six wicks using paper towels. Take a sheet of paper towel, cut it in half, fold it in half lengthwise, fold lengthwise again, then twist.

4. Place your first wick in your first container, so that the end is in the water. Bend the wick and place the other end in the second container. Place one end of your second wick in your second container, and bend it so the other end touches the water in the third container. Repeat.

5. Now wait for your rainbow bridge to form.

# The science

Your rainbow bridge is formed as the water travels up the paper towel by a process called capillary action. This is the ability of a liquid to flow upward, against gravity, in narrow spaces. The same principle is used to help water climb from a plant's roots to its leaves. Paper towels are made from fibres called cellulose, which are found in plants. In this activity, the water flowed upwards through the tiny gaps between the cellulose fibres. These gaps act like capillary tubes, pulling the water upwards. Water is able to defy gravity in this instance due to the force of attraction between the water and the cellulose fibres. Using the process of adhesion, the water molecules cling to the cellulose fibres in the paper towel. Cohesion is responsible for the water molecules attracting to each other, meaning that, as the water moves up the tiny gaps in the paper towel fibres, the cohesion forces help to draw more water upwards. Adhesive forces between the water and cellulose, plus the cohesive forces between the water molecules, will be overcome by the gravitational forces on the weight of the water in the paper towel. When this happens, the water will stop travelling up the paper towel.

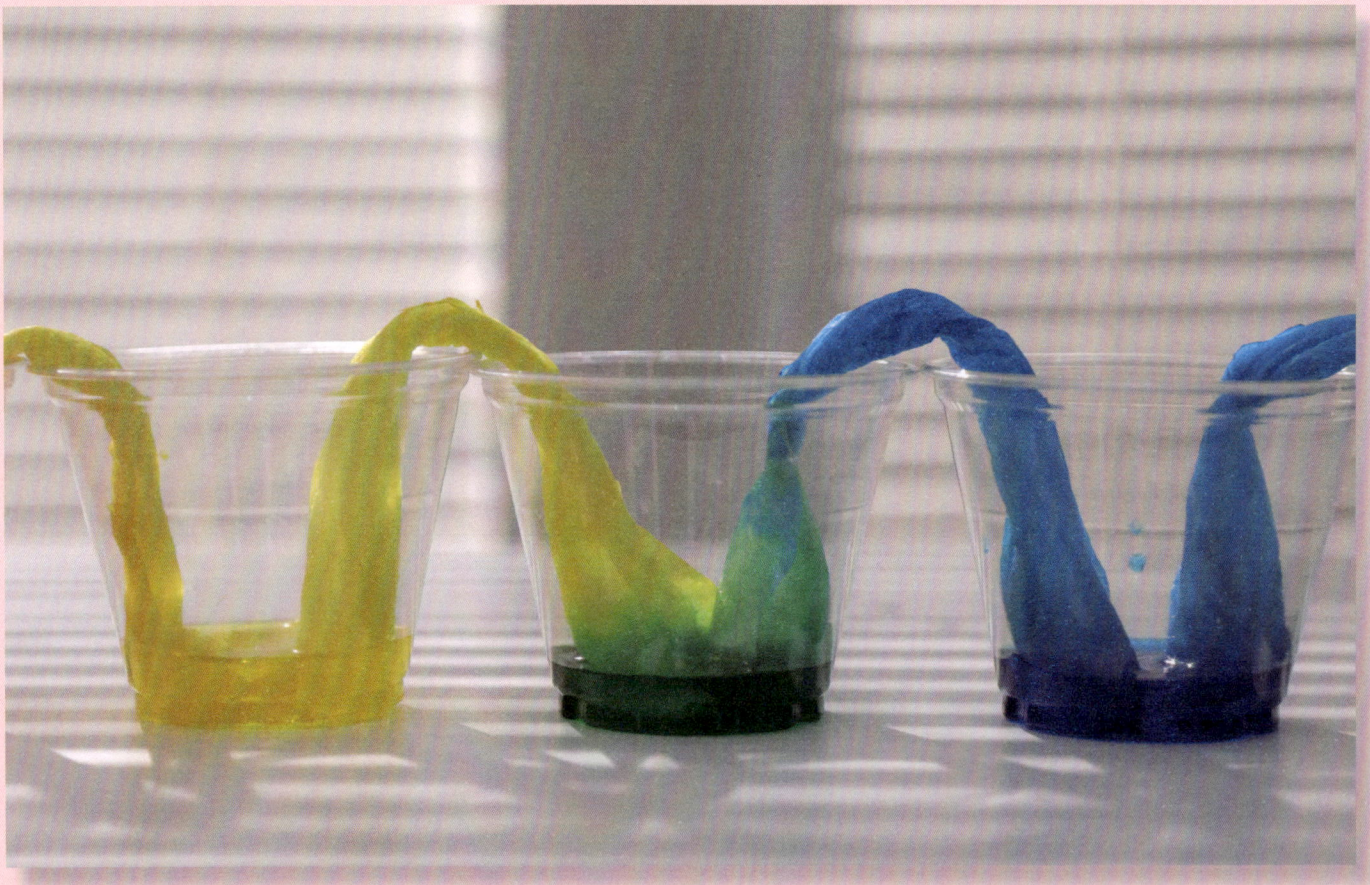

# Next level learning

Why not complete your own plant investigation to research capillary action further? Dissect a plant to take a closer look at its structure (cut flowers can work as long as they are relatively fresh). Experiment by keeping plants in different conditions (e.g. dark, light, dry soil, moist soil) and seeing what you notice.[1]

Build a bridge looking at different structures and techniques used for successful builds.

---

1  For inspiration and growing kits, see: https://www.plantletculture.com/.

Grab a microscope and study the structure of the paper towel. What do you see?

Investigate different types of paper – for example, toilet paper, newspaper, pages from a magazine. Alter the length and thickness of the paper. Vary the volume of water that you start with and see how long it takes the water to reach the empty glass.

# Making curriculum links

| EYFS | Active learning, playing and exploring, thinking critically, using materials, experimenting with colour, fine motor skills, managing self, attention and understanding. |
|------|------|
| Primary | Reading and following instructions, mathematics, working scientifically, recording results, forces, materials, colour mixing, everyday materials, living things and plants. |
| Secondary | Working scientifically, recording results, experimental skills and investigation, analysis and evaluation, measurement, structure and function of living things, forces, materials and transport systems. |

# Activity 3
# Blow art

**You will need**
- 1 x protective surface
- 1 x container
- 1 x straw
- Paint
- Water
- Paper (or card)

## The instructions

1. Mix equal quantities of paint and water in your container.

2. Place your paper on a protective surface.

3. Dip one end of your straw into your paint container, making sure it is submerged in the watered-down paint. Put your finger over the other end of the straw.

4. With your finger still over the end of the straw, carefully lift it out of the container and hold it over your paper.

5. Remove your finger from the end of the straw. Watch as the paint lands on the paper.

# The science

Wet paint is a liquid that moves around easily and drips. Watch the paint change colour and texture as it dries. The coloured particles are in a solution of either water or oil (paints can be either water- or oil-based). When exposed to air, the solvent (the liquid – in this case water or oil) begins to evaporate, leaving behind the particles. The solvent changes the way in which the light is reflected from the particles. Once the paint is dry, the colour can appear different.

# Next level learning

Experiment with different colours and mix them together.

Use the power of air to move your paint by blowing through the straw. What happens to the paint as you blow it differently – for example, harder, softer, shorter or longer breaths? Make observations about the differences between wet and dry paint.

Try dropping your paint onto the paper from different heights. What effect does this have?

Experiment with different types of paper and card.

Investigate different thicknesses of paint. Calculate the best paint-to-water ratio.

Investigate how paint is made. What chemical processes are involved?

# Making curriculum links

| EYFS | Expressive art and design, physical development, communication and language, playing and exploring, active learning. |
|------|---------------------------------------------------------------------------------------------------------------------|
| Primary | Working scientifically, materials, forces, measurement, design and evaluation. |
| Secondary | Working scientifically, forces, pure and impure substances, materials, pressure in fluids, mathematics, art and design. |

# Activity 4
# Make your own rainbow

**Light**

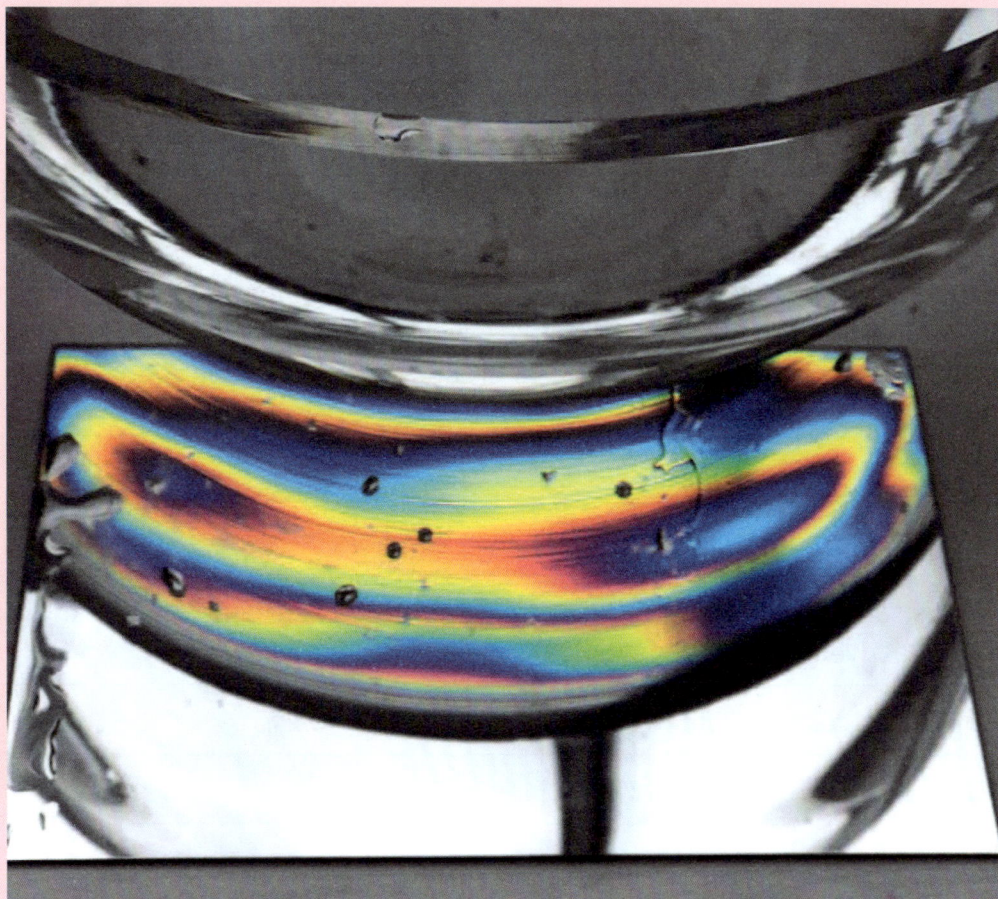

## The instructions

1. Ideally, you'll need to work in a darkened room, so turn off the lights or draw the curtains, if possible.

2. Stand your glass on the white paper.

3. Put a mirror in or under your glass making sure it is tilted slightly upwards.

4. Fill your glass with water.

5. Switch on the torch. Shine the white light from the torch through the glass onto the mirror. Watch as your rainbow appears.

## You will need

- 1 x glass
- 1 x torch
- 1 x small mirror
- White paper
- Colouring pencils
- Water

# The science

In nature, white light from the sun passes through and refracts through rain droplets to make a rainbow. The different colours that make up white light all have different wavelengths. When they are refracted through the rain droplets at different angles, their individual colours are revealed.

# Next level learning

Trace the rainbow you've created onto the white paper and label each colour. Research and create a mirror maze using light.[1]

Are you able to make a rainbow if you repeat the activity with no water in your glass?

Use a prism to split white light into the visible spectrum. Find out more about the different wavelengths and colours. Why do we see colour?[2]

Go on a rainbow hunt around your home or school. How many rainbows are you able to spot? What are the best conditions in which to spot rainbows? How are these rainbows formed? How do rainbows appear in nature? In the summer, are you able to create a rainbow using a hosepipe?

# Making curriculum links

| EYFS | Physical skills, communication, colours, drawing, learning about the world around you, active learning, communication. |
|---|---|
| Primary | Weather, colours, light, angles. |
| Secondary | Colour, light, energy, working scientifically, waves, reflection and refraction. |

---

1  For an example, see: https://www.science-sparks.com/science-fair-projects-light-maze/.
2  See: https://www.science-sparks.com/rainbow-with-a-prism/.

# Activity 5
# Rainbow trail

**Colour**

### You will need

- 1 x camera (optional)
- Paper (optional)
- Coloured crayons or pens (optional)

## The instructions

1. This activity is a bit different as you are going to go on a rainbow hunt – you will mainly need your powers of observation. Pick an area to explore. It could be a room in your home or school, or an area outside. Your challenge is to find an object that represents each colour of the rainbow – for example, the blue of the sky, the green of the grass, and the yellow of a dandelion.

2. Take a photograph or draw each of your findings to create your very own object rainbow.

## The science

Perhaps you noticed that plants come in different colours and shades. Chlorophyll is green and is responsible for the colour of a plant's foliage and leaves. Importantly, by enabling plants to produce oxygen using photosynthesis, chlorophyll is critical to sustaining life on earth. The colour comes from a plant's hereditary genome, which, in turn, determines the pigment of the plant.

If you did a nature walk during the autumn, perhaps you noticed that the leaves of certain trees were turning yellow, red or brown. This is due to changes in the temperature and the amount of daylight hours. The leaves stop making food and the chlorophyll breaks down, causing the green colour to disappear. This allows the other pigments to show through. We call these trees deciduous. Some species keep their leaves and stay green all year round; we call these evergreen.

# Next level learning

Complete your own investigation into the chemistry of the colours of autumn leaves.

Investigate photosynthesis and the chemistry of the atmosphere. What are you able to find out? How will you present your findings? Can you produce a scientific report?

What other objects did you find to make your rainbow? Investigate the different materials that they are made from.

Arrange the objects in the shape of a rainbow. Are you able to create 2D and 3D rainbows using the objects that you have found?

# Making curriculum links

| EYFS | Communication and language, understanding the world, exploring, active learning, speaking, listening and understanding, drawing, craft, creativity. |
| --- | --- |
| Primary | Plants, photosynthesis, everyday materials and their properties, seasonal changes, living things and their habitats, light. |
| Secondary | Working scientifically, cells, gas-exchange systems, reproduction, photosynthesis, ecosystems, genetics and evolution, chemical reactions, materials, Earth and atmosphere, light. |

# Activity 6
# Rainbow indicator

## Acids and alkalis

### You will need

- 1 x sieve
- 1 x pan
- 1 x hob
- 1 x bowl
- 1 x jug
- 1 x knife
- 1 x chopping board
- 1 x spoon
- 3 x small containers
- Water
- Red cabbage
- Lemon juice
- Baking soda
- Washing powder

This activity involves knives and boiling water. Depending on the age of the learners, an adult could prepare the indicator in advance. Close supervision is essential when working with acids and alkalis.

# The instructions

1. Carefully chop two large leaves of red cabbage into small pieces. Place it in a pan, cover with water and boil for ten minutes.

2. Drain the cabbage through a sieve making sure to collect the water in a bowl. The cabbage will have dyed this water purple – this will become your indicator. Set the indicator aside and wait for it to cool, then pour it into a jug.

3. Add a small amount of lemon juice to one container. In another container, mix a spoon of baking soda with a spoon of fresh water (not your indicator solution). In your final container, combine a spoon of washing powder with a spoon of fresh water.

4. Pour a small amount of indicator into each container. Watch as each of the household substances changes colour.

# The science

Red cabbage contains anthocyanins, which change colour when they come into contact with acids or alkalis. You will have noted that when the indicator was added to the lemon juice, the solution turned red. This indicates an acid. Washing powder is an alkali, so turns green when the indicator is added. Baking soda turns blue. Acidic solutions have a pH of less than 7 and alkali solutions have a pH of more than 7.

# Next level learning

Investigate the pH scale. What other indicators are available? What are they used for and how do they work?

Choose some other household substances to test. Have fun with some scientific magic using the indicator to change their colour and see if they are acid or alkali. Are you able to create a rainbow when testing household substances?

# Making curriculum links

| EYFS | Active learning, understanding the world, playing and exploring, expressive arts, investigating colour change, creating and thinking critically. |
| --- | --- |
| Primary | Working scientifically, materials. |
| Secondary | Chemical changes, working scientifically, chemical reactions, acids and alkalis. |

# Activity 7
# Floating rainbow

## You will need

- 1 x ceramic plate
- 1 x jug of water
- Whiteboard pens

## The instructions

1. Draw a rainbow on your plate with your whiteboard pens. Aim to keep the shapes as simple as possible.

2. Pour the water from your jug onto the plate. Take care not to pour too fast.

3. Watch as the water starts to lift your picture from the plate and bring your rainbow to life!

## The science

As you make your drawing on the smooth surface of the plate, the oily silicone polymer in the white-board pen prevents it from sticking to the surface. You will have observed your drawing 'magically' detach from the surface of the plate and rise to the surface of the water. Here it floats. This is because the ink is lighter (less dense) than the water. Whiteboard pens contain a solvent used to dissolve the pigments that determine the pen's colour. A polymer is added to ensure that the ink is erasable. This is what makes the ink slippery, preventing it from sticking to the whiteboard – and to your plate.

## Next level learning

Why not investigate polymers further? What are the many uses of polymers? Why do whiteboard pens stain clothes but not a whiteboard? What is the difference between a permanent marker and a dry-wipe pen?

What other pictures are you able to create? Which colours work best? Challenge yourself to make an object 'walk' across the plate. Are you able to pick your drawing up from the surface of the water?

## Making curriculum links

| EYFS | Active learning, expressive art, listening and communication, understanding, moving and handling, exploring media and materials, being imaginative. |
|---|---|
| Primary | Working scientifically, materials. |
| Secondary | Working scientifically, materials, solvents, polymers, chemistry, matter. |

# Activity 8
# Chromatography art

## Chromatography

### You will need

- 1 x small container
- Felt tip pens
- Filter paper (e.g. coffee filter)
- Water
- Scissors
- Glue
- Paper or card

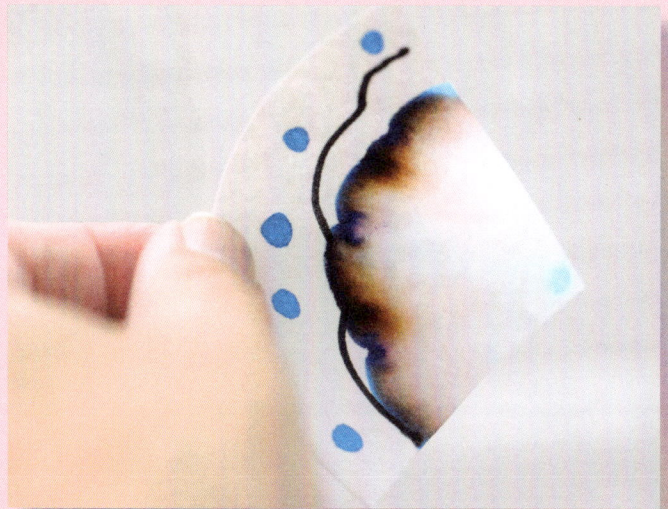

## The instructions

1. Cut your filter paper into strips or segments of a size of your choosing. Using a felt tip pen (black or brown works well), add a spot of colour approximately 2 cm from the base of the piece of filter paper. If you want to, you can get really creative, adding patterns. Add colour to as many pieces as you like.

2. Fill a small container with a small amount of water.

3. Add a piece of filter paper to the container, allowing only the very bottom of it to touch the water.

4. Watch carefully as the water moves up the paper via capillary action, separating the colours in the ink.

5. Carefully remove the filter paper from the water, leaving aside to dry.

6. Repeat steps 3-5 with your remaining pieces of filter paper.

7. Now it's time to get creative. What will your chromatography become? A unicorn's mane? A firework? Part of a rainbow? It really is up to you. Cut out your chromatography sample, gluing it to your paper or card, and create a piece of art around it.

# The science

The ink in felt tip pens often is not a single colour but is made up of several colourful chemicals. When water soaks into the filter paper, using capillary action, it dissolves some of the ink molecules and carries them with it. The bigger, heavier molecules in the ink don't move as far as the smaller, lighter ones. Different molecules move with the water at different speeds, settling in different places as the water travels upwards. Darker inks like black and brown work best in this activity as they tend to be made of many more colours.

# Next level learning

Investigate the different types of chromatography. Find out about its real-world application – when, how and why is it used?

Complete a full investigation into how paper chromatography can be used to separate and identify different coloured substances. Measure the distance travelled by each spot and by the solvent, calculating the retardation factor (Rf value) of each spot. This is the ratio of the distance moved by the solute to the distance moved by the solvent.

Turn your chromatography into 3D artworks. Create an exhibition in school or online to showcase your work.

# Making curriculum links

| EYFS | Active learning, expressive arts and design, physical development, fine motor skills. |
|------|---------------------------------------------------------------------------------------|
| Primary | Art and design, properties of materials, material changes, working scientifically. |
| Secondary | Chemical analysis, working scientifically, pure and impure substances, separation techniques, analysing and identifying substances, calculations. |

# Activity 9
# Bubbles

**Surface tension**

**You will need**

- 1 x tray
- Bubble solution (ready to use or homemade)
- Pipe cleaners

Be wary of surfaces becoming slippery. To minimise the mess, make your bubbles in a tray or outside.

# The instructions

1. Pour your bubble solution into your tray. If you do not have bubble solution, try mixing washing up liquid or baby shampoo with water. You'll need 500 ml of water to 500 ml of baby shampoo or washing up liquid, plus 10 ml of glycerine. Glycerine makes the bubbles last longer. Mix the ingredients together and allow the mixture to stand before use.

2. Make bubble wands by twisting pipe cleaners into different shapes – for example, a triangle, a heart, a square, or maybe even a butterfly.

3. Experiment by blowing bubbles with your different bubble wands. What do you notice? Does the bubble created match the shape of the wand?

# The science

As you play with your bubbles, you'll notice that when it's floating in the air, a bubble becomes a sphere, but the soap film on the bubble wand is flat. Soap films are made from soap and water. Bubbles are soap films wrapped around air. The shape of bubbles is predictable, as it takes energy to deform a bubble. They tend to spring back into shape to occupy the minimal surface. This explains why all free-floating bubbles are spheres, as a sphere has the least surface area for a given volume of air.

# Next level learning

Have a go at producing giant bubbles.

Make 3D bubble wands and see what happens.

Why does soap create a film? Do some research or an investigation and write up your findings.

Compare bubble elasticity with other objects (e.g. an elastic band).

Investigate surface structures.

Make bubble prints using paint and card.

## Making curriculum links

| EYFS | Understanding the world, listening and attention, communication, physical development, active learning, imagination, playing and exploring. |
| --- | --- |
| Primary | Working scientifically, forces, materials. |
| Secondary | Technology, art and design, structure of matter, forces, energy, coordination and control, working scientifically, ratios. |

# Activity 10
# Universe in a jar

**Capillary action**

## You will need

- 1 x jar
- 1 x jug
- Food colouring (at least two different colours)
- Biodegradable glitter
- Cotton wool balls
- Water
- Spoon

# The instructions

1. Add some water to your jar, then add a couple of drops of your first chosen food colouring. Mix well, then add some biodegradable glitter.

2. Separate your cotton wool balls into long pieces and divide them into two batches.

3. Add the first batch of cotton wool to your jar. The cotton wool will start to compress and absorb the water, so a little patience is required. Once the water is absorbed, fill the jar with the remaining cotton wool.

4. In your jug, mix water and biodegradable glitter with your second choice of food colouring. Pour the mixture into the jar. Enjoy your universe in a jar!

# The science

Cotton is a plant fibre that contains cellulose. Cellulose has hydrophilic properties - 'hydro' meaning 'water' and '-philic' meaning 'loving'. This means that the structure of the cotton attracts the water molecules. Another process involved here is capillary action, which sucks water into the fibres and stores it. The fluid fills the narrow spaces within the structure of the material. The colour in this experiment means that you can more easily see the water being absorbed.

# Next level learning

What will your universe be called? Where will your universe be located? Why not research the galaxy we live in. How would you travel into space? What resources would you need? Are you able to build a mode of transport plus living quarters?

What will happen to the jar when you have finished with your universe? Why is it important to reuse and recycle materials?

Try different colour combinations. Which colours work best together? Do different colours behave differently?

# Making curriculum links

| EYFS | Expressive arts and design, exploring media and mediums, active learning, understanding the world, imagination. |
| --- | --- |
| Primary | Everyday materials, Earth and space, capillary action, materials and their properties. |
| Secondary | Earth and space, capillary action, materials and their properties. |

# Activity 11
# Over the rainbow magnet maze

**Magnetism**

## You will need

- 1 x paper plate
- 1 x magnet
- 1 x piece of card
- 1 x pencil
- Felt tip pens
- Scissors
- Metal paperclips

**Adult supervision is essential when using scissors.**

## The instructions

1. Using felt tip pens, draw a rainbow maze on your paper plate. Be creative and let your imagination run wild.

2. Using your card and pencil, design a character to fly over your rainbow maze. Colour in your character and, with adult permission, carefully cut them out. Attach the paper clip to your character and place them at the start of rainbow maze.

3. Put your magnet underneath the paper plate and position it so it attracts the paper clip. Move your magnet under the rainbow and watch your character fly!

# The science

Magnets have two poles: north and south. The poles are the parts where the magnetic force is strongest. Around these poles is an area known as a magnetic field. For an object to be drawn to the magnet, it has to be within its magnetic field. A magnet can control another object without even touching it, but it won't work on every material. Your character wouldn't move without the metal paperclip, as paper and card are not magnetic. Iron, nickel and cobalt are magnetic elements. Alloys containing these metals are also magnetic – for example, steel contains iron.

# Next level learning

How are magnets useful in our everyday lives? How and when are magnets used in real-world situations? What real-world problem could you use a magnet to solve?

Which elements are magnetic? Why do you think this is?

Investigate the magnetic properties of different materials. Test around your home or school to see which items are magnetic and which are not.

Are you able to construct a 3D magnet maze?

# Making curriculum links

| EYFS | Active learning, understanding the world, imagination, playing and exploring. |
|------|-------------------------------------------------------------------------------|
| Primary | Everyday materials, forces and magnets. |
| Secondary | Magnetism, forces, elements, metals, materials and their properties. |

# Activity 12
# Colour changing water

Colour

## You will need

- 1 x large clear jug
- 1 x clear glass
- 1 x large clear bowl
- 1 x spoon
- Water
- Food colouring (yellow and blue)

## The instructions

1. Add water to your glass until it is three-quarters full. Add a couple of drops of blue food colouring to the water, stirring until it is fully combined.

2. Fill your jug with water. Add a few drops of yellow food colouring, stirring until it is fully combined.

3. Place your glass of blue water in the middle of your empty bowl.

4. Carefully pour the yellow water from the jug into the bowl, making sure not to splash any into the blue water. What do you notice?

# The science

Red, blue and yellow are primary colours. When you combine these colours in equal amounts, white light is produced. When they are combined in different amounts, they produce secondary colours. The secondary colours are orange, green and purple. The primary colours blue and yellow are used in this experiment to make the secondary colour green.

# Next level learning

What happens if you try this experiment using other colours? Why not try red and yellow, or red and blue? How many colours do you see? Is it different from what you started with? What do you think will happen if you remove the glass from the bowl?

Experiment using different volumes of coloured water. What are you able to find out?

# Making curriculum links

| EYFS | Active learning, understanding the world, creative and critical thinking, understanding, imagination, exploring colours. |
| --- | --- |
| Primary | Everyday materials, colour mixing, working scientifically, working creatively, evaluating and testing ideas, mathematics. |
| Secondary | Light, colour, working scientifically, mathematics, pressure in fluids. |

# Activity 13
# Rainbow in a jar

## Density - Solutions

**You will need**

- 1 x jar
- 1 x jug
- 1 x teaspoon
- Food colouring (red, yellow, green, blue)
- Sugar
- Warm water (same volume for each colour dependent upon size of container)

## The instructions

1. Add eight teaspoons of sugar to a jug. Cover the sugar with enough warm water to allow it to dissolve. Once fully dissolved, add the blue food colouring and stir. Add the blue sugar solution to your jar. Leave to settle.

2. Rinse out your jug, then add six teaspoons of sugar. Again, dissolve it in warm water, but add green food colouring this time. Carefully add the solution to your jar and leave to settle.

3. Rinse out your jug, and add four teaspoons of sugar. Once again, dissolve it in warm water before adding yellow food colouring this time. Carefully add the solution to your jar and leave to settle.

4. Rinse out your jug. Finally, mix warm water with red food colouring. Complete your rainbow by adding this to the jar.

# The science

The more sugar, the greater the density of the solution. The denser the substance, the more likely it is to sink; therefore, we are able to create our rainbow sugar water density column. Varying the amount of sugar but keeping the volume of water constant creates solutions of different densities. The more sugar mixed in the water, the higher the density, creating the stacking effect.

$$\text{density} = \frac{\text{mass}}{\text{volume}}$$

# Next level learning

What are the units used to measure density? Why do substances have different densities? Think about the atomic density of solids, liquids and gases. How does atomic structure affect density? Investigate the density values of everyday substances – for example, water, air and steel.

Work on the sugar-to-water ratio to form the perfect rainbow in your jar. What happens if you use a container that is a different size or shape? Are you able to design a container to really show off your rainbow?

# Making curriculum links

| EYFS | Active learning, understanding the world, creative and critical thinking, exploring colours, imagination. |
|------|------------------------------------------------------------------------------------------------------------|
| Primary | Everyday materials, colour mixing, working scientifically, working creatively, evaluating and testing ideas, mathematics. |
| Secondary | Light, colour, working scientifically, mathematics, pressure in fluids, density, particular nature of matter, solubility, atomic structure, ratio, physical changes. |

# Activity 14
# Rainbow density column

**Colour – Density**

## You will need

- 1 x test tube or jar
- 7 x containers
- 7 x different liquids of different densities (e.g. ketchup, golden syrup, toothpaste, hand soap, milk, honey, cooking oil, water)
- Food colouring (red, orange, yellow, green, blue, indigo, violet)

# The instructions

1. The heaviest liquid will need to be added to the test tube or jar first. This is the one with the highest density. Why not do an investigation to see which of your liquids is the heaviest?

2. In a container, mix the heaviest liquid with the colour that you want at the bottom of your density column. In this case, the toothpaste with the purple food colouring. Add the mixture to the test tube or jar. Take your time, allowing each layer to settle before adding the next one.

3. Continue by mixing the next colour with the next heaviest liquid. Add the mixture to the test tube or jar. Try to use the same amount of liquid in each layer.

4. Repeat steps 2-3 until the test tube or jar is full and your rainbow is complete. Leave to settle and enjoy your rainbow density column.

# The science

You will see the liquids stack on top of each other in layers. This is because the liquids have different densities, so don't mix together. Some of the liquids repel each other, so do not mix - for example, oil and water - others resist mixing because they are so viscous (or thick).

You were able to stack your liquids using the science of density. Density is the measure of how much mass is contained within a given volume, or, in other words, how much 'stuff' there is and how tightly packed together this 'stuff' is! You are able to calculate density using the following equation:

$$\text{density} = \frac{\text{mass}}{\text{volume}}$$

If the mass of something increases but the volume stays the same, the density has to go up. If the mass decreases but the volume stays the same, the density has to go down. Lighter liquids - for example, water - are less dense or have less 'stuff' packed into them than heavier liquids - for example, honey.

# Next level learning

Each liquid has a different density, which can be measured as grams per cubic centimetre (g/cm$^3$). Why not investigate densities further? Are you able to work out the ideal volume of each liquid to create the perfect density column in the container that you are using?

Are you able to identify liquids to create your density column using all of the colours of the rainbow without the need for food colouring? Are you able to discover their individual densities to make sure they stack in the colour order of the rainbow?

Get creative and select small items from around the home or school – for example, a key, a rubber bouncy ball, a blueberry. Carefully drop each item into the centre of your density column. Observe and record what happens. Some items will stay on or near the top and others will sink part or all of the way down the density column. The densities and masses of the objects you drop into the density column will vary. If the layer of liquid is denser than the object itself, the object stays on top of that liquid. If the layer of liquid is less dense than the object, the object sinks until it meets a liquid layer that is dense enough to hold it.

Have a viscosity race with different liquids. Why do different liquids travel at different speeds?

# Making curriculum links

| EYFS | Exploring colours, active learning, understanding the world, creative and critical thinking, imagination. |
|---|---|
| Primary | Colour, everyday materials, working scientifically, working creatively, evaluating and testing ideas, mathematics. |
| Secondary | Working scientifically, mathematics, pressure in fluids, density, particular nature of matter, atomic structure. |

# Activity 15
# Rainbow flowers

**Capillary action**

Be extremely careful when cutting flowers.

## You will need

- 1 x cutting board
- 1 x container
- 1 x white flower (or celery as an alternative)
- Food colouring or ink
- Water
- Scissors

## The instructions

1. Add water to your container and mix in your food colouring or ink.

2. Trim the stem of a flower and add it to the water. Wait and observe as the petals begin to change colour.

# The science

Plants require water to survive. They take water from the ground and transport it to the leaves using a process called capillary action. Water evaporates from the leaves causing a pressure change in the stem - in a process called transpiration - and liquid to be drawn up from the roots. In this case, the water is dyed and this is why the flower changes colour.

# Next level learning

Are you able to make a rainbow flower? To do this, you will need to carefully split the stem of a flower into seven parts and add each one to a container filled with different coloured water.[1]

Which flowers work best? Complete an investigation into this. Does the age of the cut flower play a part in your success?

Are you able to speed up the process of transpiration? What effect does this have on your investigation? Dissect your flower to take a closer look. Are you able to identify all the different parts of the flower, including the ones responsible for allowing the colour change?

Keep a diary of observations to record what is happening to your flowers on a daily basis. Create a colourful comic strip, storyboard or factsheet to explain your observations to others.

---

1   For an example, see: https://www.thoughtco.com/how-to-make-a-rainbow-rose-606168.

## Making curriculum links

| Nursery | Imagination, playing and exploring, learning colours, communication. |
|---------|----------------------------------------------------------------------|
| EYFS | Colour, active learning, understanding the world, creative and critical thinking. |
| Primary | Colour, working scientifically, working creatively, evaluating and testing ideas. |
| Secondary | Working scientifically, capillary action, plant biology. |

# Activity 16
# Colourful plant growth

## The instructions

1. Add compost to your test tubes and add the pea seeds. (You can also use a nutrient-rich gel as the growing medium, as shown in the pictures.[2])

2. Wrap a different coloured filter around each test tube, securing with tape or glue. Your clear filter will act as your control.

3. Place the seeds in direct sunlight, keeping them in the same location throughout the experiment.

4. Water your peas and measure their growth daily, with the ruler. Record your results by creating a growth chart using your pencil and ruler.

5. Continue to do this for at least two weeks.

## You will need

- 1 x 30 cm ruler
- 1 x pencil
- 1 x clear plastic filter
- 4 x coloured filters (red, green, blue, yellow)
- 5 x test tubes (or small plant pots)
- Pea seeds[1]
- Compost
- Tape or glue
- Paper

## The science

The relationship between light and plant growth can be observed by exposing your peas to different coloured light. Plants require light to carry out photosynthesis (the process of making energy in leaves). Leaves are most able to utilise red, blue and yellow light.

This investigation will help you discover whether the colour of a greenhouse impacts the growth of the plants inside. Plants are commonly grown in greenhouses to provide extra warmth and humidity, allowing them to thrive to increase crop production and meet consumer demand. This method also extends the plants' growing season, meaning we can produce even when the conditions are not ideal outside (e.g. too cold).

## Next level learning

Are plants able to transform light into energy when colours are missing from the visible-light spectrum? What colours do plants need to gain energy from sunlight?

Further investigate how plants use chlorophyll. How do plants convert sunlight into energy?

---

1   For the best results, these will need to be pre-soaked and starting to germinate.

2   Available from: https://www.plantletculture.com/.

What are the dependent and independent variables in this investigation? Which variables will you need to control and why is this important?

How would increasing the number of peas improve the reliability of your results?

Are you able to produce a full scientific report making recommendations to plant growers and crop producers based on your evidence about the best colour light for growing plants in greenhouses?

Do different plants react differently in different colours of light? Repeat the experiment with a variety of different vegetables.

Start to think about greenhouse design and innovation for the future. Are you able to construct your own mini greenhouses? Investigate how this experiment links to a future career in food production, farming, horticulture, food technology or business.

# Making curriculum links

| EYFS | Exploring colours, active learning, understanding the world, critical thinking, imagination. |
| --- | --- |
| Primary | Plants, living things, colour, light, working scientifically, working creatively, evaluating and testing ideas, mathematics, measuring. |
| Secondary | Working scientifically, mathematics, design and technology, plant biology, photosynthesis, colour. |

# Activity 17
# Rainbow lava lamps

## Density

### You will need

- 1 x jar
- 1 x spoon
- 1 x small container
- Baby oil
- White vinegar
- Food colouring
- Baking soda

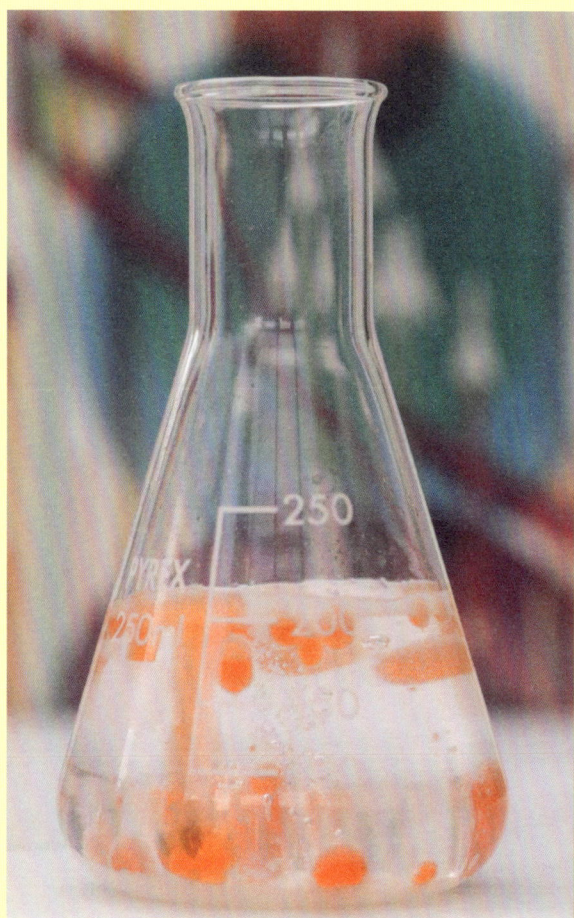

## The instructions

1. Add the baking soda to your jar. Precise quantities don't matter, but it needs to be enough to cover the base of the jar with a thin layer.

2. Add the oil to your jar. Make sure the layer of oil is deep enough for you to be able to see the lava lamp reaction. Leave to settle.

3. In another small container, mix the vinegar and food colouring (any colour you want) until completely combined.

4. Slowly pour your vinegar and food colouring solution into your jar. Watch as the reaction creates the effect of a lava lamp.

## The science

Oil and vinegar are different densities. As vinegar is denser than the oil, it sinks to the bottom of the container. When the vinegar reaches the bottom, it reacts with the baking soda. This chemical reaction releases bubbling carbon dioxide gas. Gas rises, creating the lava lamp effect.

## Next level learning

Research gas tests. How will you prove that carbon dioxide gas was produced? Are you able to measure and record the volume of gas produced in the reaction? Which factors influence this? Complete a full investigation stating your variables. Why are variables important? Present your findings using graphs.

Are you able to write out the word and chemical equations associated with this experiment? Can you balance this equation?

Investigate the effect of different containers – and different quantities of baking soda, vinegar and baby oil – to create the ultimate lava lamp. What will your measures be? The number of bubbles created? The speed at which the bubbles travel? The duration of the reaction? Complete a report detailing your findings and do not forget to record them in a results table. Are you able to recommend the best lava lamp design to others?

Create a full rainbow of lava lamps all reacting at the same time. Try illuminating your lava lamps with a torch.

Investigate gasses, density and chemical reactions.

How might you be able to use the skills learnt in this activity in a future career? When might they be useful? How does this chemistry relate to industry?

# Making curriculum links

| EYFS | Exploring colours, active learning, understanding the world, critical thinking, imagination. |
| --- | --- |
| Primary | Colour, light, everyday materials, working scientifically, working creatively, evaluating and testing ideas, mathematics, art and design, states of matter, properties of materials. |
| Secondary | Working scientifically, mathematics, design and technology, colour, light, nature of matter, gas tests, chemical reactions, the periodic table, materials, energy changes and transfers, changes in systems, pressure in fluids, chemical changes. |

# Activity 18
# Rainbow cloud

## You will need

- 1 x jar
- 7 x pipettes
- 7 x small containers
- Shaving foam (cream, not gel)
- Food colouring (red, orange, yellow, green, blue, indigo, violet)
- Water

# The instructions

1. In a small container, mix water with a few drops of red food colouring. Repeat this with each colour of the rainbow. (Or you can use whichever colours you have to hand.) Place a pipette into each of your coloured water containers. If you don't have pipettes, you could use spoons or straws.

2. Fill your jar three-quarters full of fresh water. Carefully spray shaving foam on top of the water. You want to create a 'cloud' that sits on top of the water and pokes out just above the top of the jar.

3. Collect the first coloured water sample with the pipette, adding this to the top of the shaving foam cloud. Repeat with each colour.

4. Look closely to see what is happening below the cloud. The colours will start to seep through the shaving foam and appear in the water in the jar, creating your rainbow.

# The science

Imagine that the shaving foam is your cloud and the water below it is the air. The coloured water is your rainbow. The coloured water saturates the cloud, causing it to get heavier. Eventually it becomes so heavy that the cloud is no longer able to hold the water, creating your rainbow as the colours rain down into the jar. This represents how rain falls through the air.

# Next level learning

Prior to completing the experiment, are you able to make a hypothesis about what you think will happen? Record what you observe as the experiment is completed, then write a conclusion linking your hypothesis with the results.

Investigate the weather and how rain and rainbows are formed in nature.

# Making curriculum links

| EYFS | Exploring colours, active learning, understanding the world, observation and communication, imagination. |
|------|---------------------------------------------------------------------------------------------------------|
| Primary | Weather, working scientifically, working creatively, evaluating and testing ideas, Earth. |
| Secondary | Working scientifically, colour, light, nature of matter, scientific method. |

# Activity 19
# Colour shadows

## You will need

- 1 x dark room
- 1 x pencil
- 1 x white wall or screen
- 3 x coloured filters (red, green, blue)
- 3 x torches
- Scissors
- Books
- Plasticine
- Tape

Take care when using scissors.

# The instructions

1. Place the bulb end of a torch on a coloured filter and draw around it. Carefully cut out a piece of coloured filter that is slightly larger than the torch. Using tape, attach the filter to the torch. Repeat this step so your three torches each have a different coloured filter.

2. Using books as supports, place the three torches so that they shine together on your white wall or screen.

3. Stand your pencil between the torches and the wall, using the plasticine to secure it in place. Turn on one torch and observe as the pencil casts a shadow.

4. Now switch on all three of the torches. Observe what happens to the shadow.

5. Now turn off differing combinations of the three torches, observing what colour shadow the pencil casts.

# The science

Light is a spectrum of all the wavelengths that can be detected by the eye. The RGB cones of the eye are most sensitive to red, green and blue wavelengths. These three cones overlap to allow us to perceive all visible colours.

How did the coloured filters work? When red, blue and green light trigger the three colour receptors on our retinas equally, the signals combine in the brain so we can see white light. In this investigation, the coloured filters block some wavelengths but allow others through. The red filtered torch shows wavelengths from red to orange and yellow. The green filtered torch displays yellow, green and blue, and the blue filtered torch shows green, blue and purple. You were able to see white light when all three torches were shone together because you observed the wavelengths red to purple.

# Next level learning

Suggest a real-world application for this investigation.

Use this investigation to observe and describe how different colours of light mix to give different colours. You should be able to make seven different colours: blue, red, green, black, cyan, magenta, and yellow. When you block two of the three lights you will produce a shadow of the third colour – e.g. block the red and green light and you will observe a blue shadow. Block all three lights and you will observe a black shadow.

Work out all of the different colour combinations you are able to create. Add these effects to your own mini film set or make a mini concert stage to show off your new lighting skills!

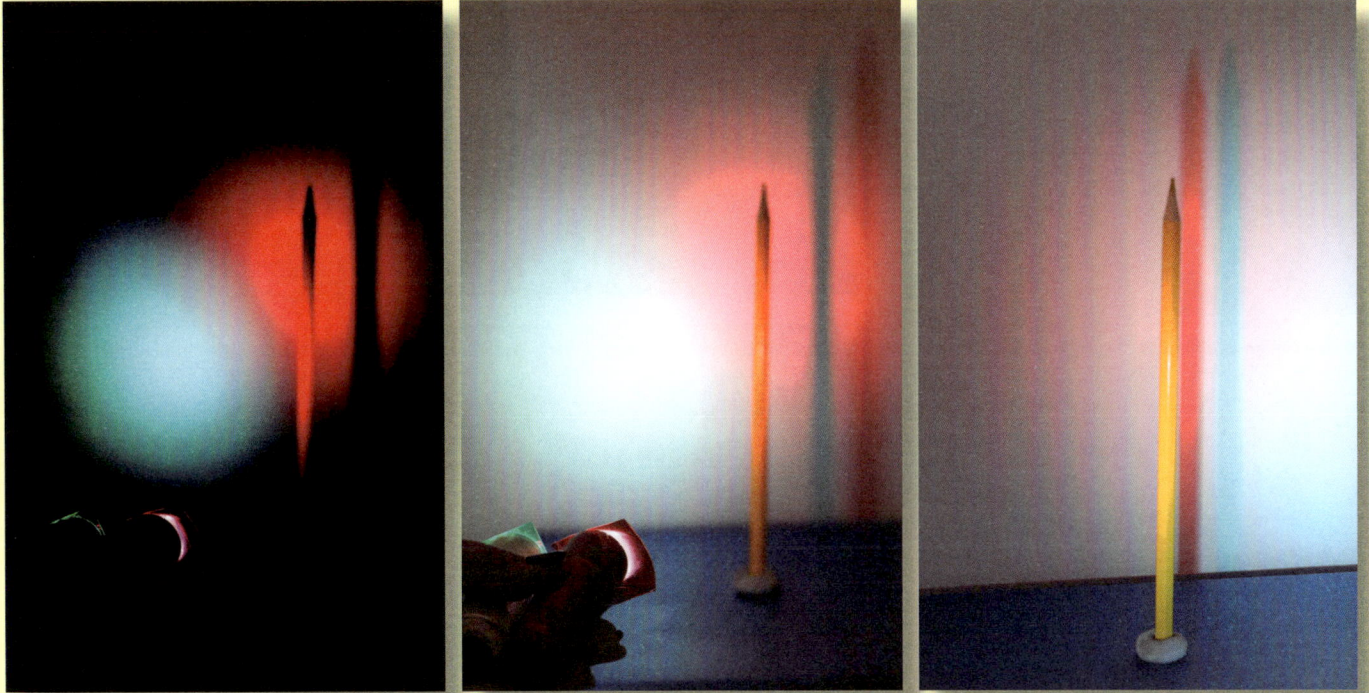

# Making curriculum links

| EYFS | Exploring colours, active learning, understanding the world, observation and communication, imagination. |
|---|---|
| Primary | Working scientifically, working creatively, evaluating and testing ideas, light, colour, human body, energy. |
| Secondary | Working scientifically, colour, light, human anatomy, energy. |

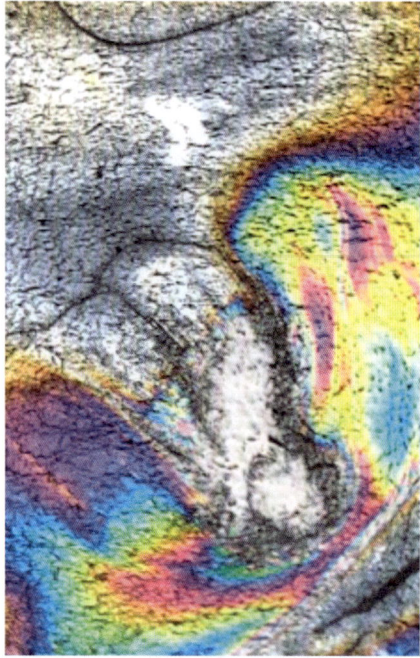

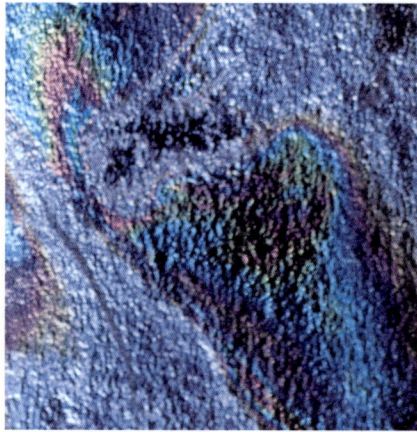

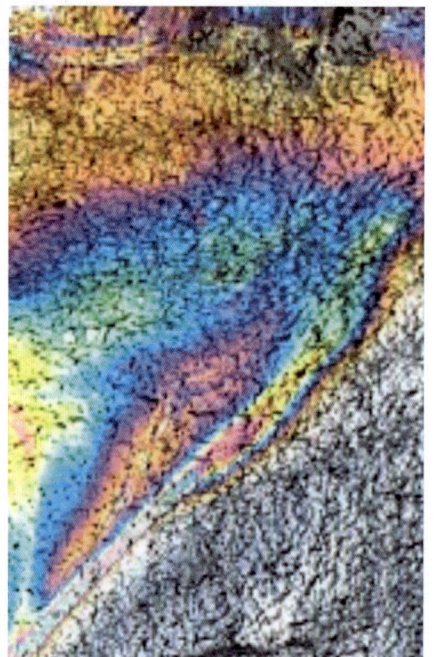

# Activity 20
# Rainbow paper

## Light – Polymers

## The instructions

1. Pour water into your shallow bowl and add a drop of clear nail polish. Observe as the polish forms a film on top of the water.

2. Carefully lay your paper on top of the water. Move it around to capture the film created by the nail polish.

3. Remove your paper and leave it to dry.

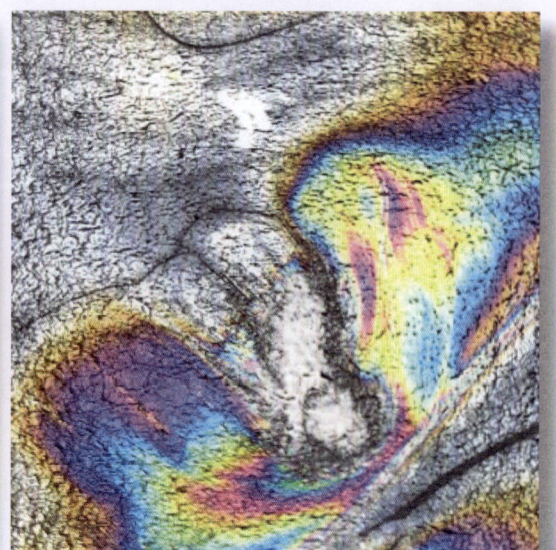

# The science

When you add the clear nail polish to the water it spreads out and polymerisation is observed. It is this action that creates the film. As white light hits the film, some of it bounces back, while other rays continue through and then bounce off the back of the paper. The light moving into the film travels further than the light reflected off the surface, creating a wave effect. You see different colours because the wavelength of the light changes.

# Next level learning

Complete a full wavelength investigation looking into why and how different colours are observed on the rainbow paper.

What happens if you experiment with paper of different colours and textures? Record your findings.

What is polymerisation and what are its real-world applications?

Get creative. Cut your rainbow paper into a variety of shapes and make some artworks.

# Making curriculum links

| EYFS | Exploring colours, active learning, shape, observation and communication, imagination. |
|---|---|
| Primary | Working scientifically, working creatively, evaluating and testing ideas, light, colour. |
| Secondary | Working scientifically, colour, light, polymerisation, materials and their properties. |

# Activity 21
# Rainbow milk

## Hydrophilic and hydrophobic molecules

## You will need

- 1 x shallow bowl
- Liquid soap
- Food colouring (the more colours, the better)
- Whole milk

## The instructions

1. Pour your milk into your shallow bowl, making sure it covers the base.

2. Add three to four drops of each food colouring to the milk.

3. Place one drop of liquid soap in the centre of the bowl.

4. Watch carefully as the colours move across the surface of the milk.

## The science

Liquid soap plays a key part in moving the colours across the surface of the milk. This is because soap molecules have water-loving (hydrophilic) and water-hating (hydrophobic) ends. Water molecules are polar molecules, but fat and oil molecules are nonpolar molecules. Fats and oils do not dissolve in water. Milk consists of water, fat, vitamins and minerals. When soap is added to the milk, it separates the water and fat. As soap is added to the milk, the hydrophobic end of the soap molecule breaks up the nonpolar fat molecules. The hydrophilic end of the soap molecule links to the polar water molecules. The soap is now connecting the water and the fat, with the nonpolar fat molecules carried by the polar water molecules. When the soap molecules connect to the fat molecules, the molecules of the food colouring are moved around, which is what creates the explosion of colour. The majority of the water molecules attach to the fat molecules as the soap spreads throughout the milk, the colour explosion will then eventually slow and stop.

# Next level learning

Further investigate hydrophobic and hydrophilic, and polar and nonpolar, molecules.

This experiment works best with whole milk as it contains more fat (roughly 4%) but why not investigate what happens when you use milk with different fat percentages? Observe how the explosion of colour alters when you use skimmed milk, semi-skimmed milk, cream or even condensed milk. Record your results and observations. What recommendations or advice would you give to someone who wanted to complete this experiment?

# Making curriculum links

| EYFS | Exploring colours, active learning, observation, communication, language, physical development, mathematics, imagination. |
|------|--------------------------------------------------------------------------------------------------------------------------|
| Primary | Working scientifically, working creatively, evaluating and testing ideas, colour, measuring, volume, counting. |
| Secondary | Working scientifically, colour, mathematics, problem solving, conceptual understanding, measurement, nutrition, molecules, polarity, experimental skills and observation. |

# Activity 22
# Rainbow ice

## Diffusion – Ionic compounds – States of matter

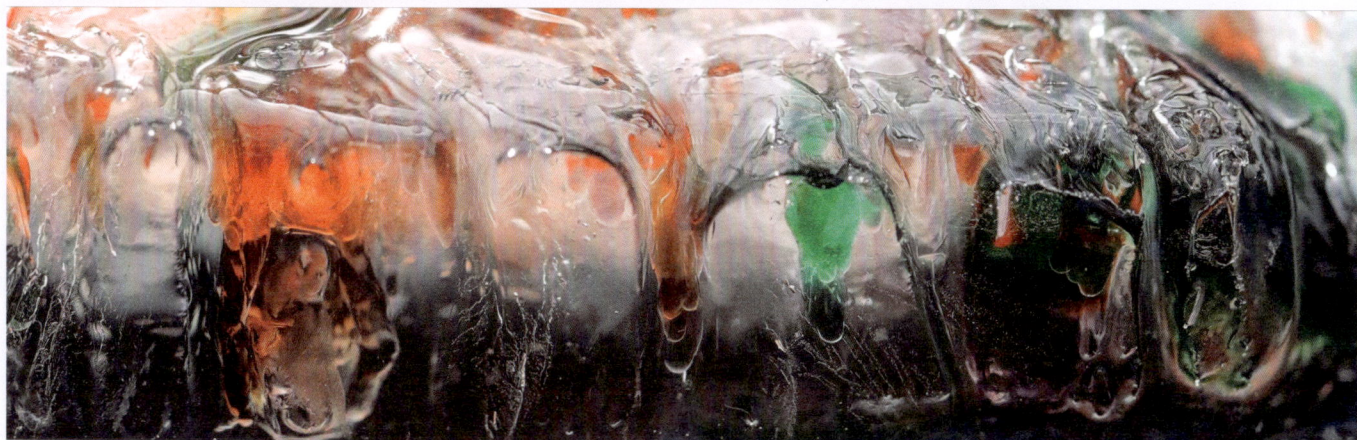

## You will need

- 1 x container
- 1 x teaspoon
- 1 x tray
- 1 x pipette
- Ice[1]
- Salt
- Food colouring
- Warm water

## The instructions

1. Fill your container with warm water and mix in five drops of food colouring. If you want to experiment with more than one colour, gather some additional containers and repeat this step for every colour you want to use.

2. Add at least five teaspoons of salt to the coloured water. The exact quantity will be dependent upon the size of the container, so keep adding until the solution is saturated with the salt.

3. Place your ice into your tray.

4. Fill your pipette with the coloured salt water. Squeeze it over the ice and watch as the salt begins to melt the ice. Watch as rivulets start to form in the block of ice, salt concentrates in different parts and little bubbles of colour start to form inside the ice.

---

1  For the best results, freeze water in containers of different sizes and shapes, so you end up with cubes and blocks.

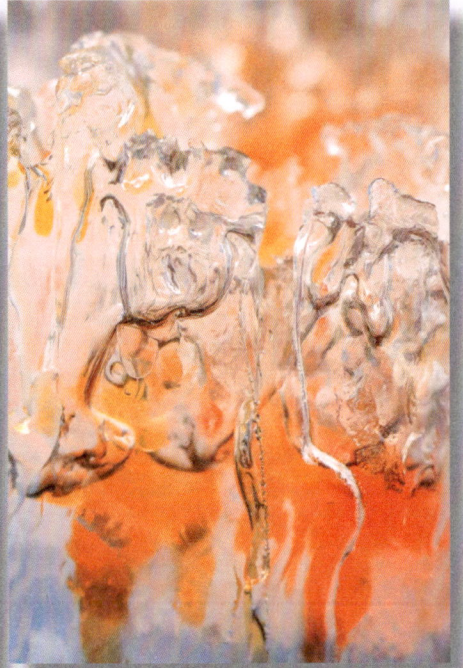

## The science

Salt contains sodium. Sodium heats up the ice causing it to slowly melt as salt water has a lower freezing point. The salt diffuses in the water creating the beautiful effects in the ice. The solution of salt and water needs to be saturated. This means that no more salt can be dissolved in the given volume of water. A weaker solution won't be as effective at melting the ice. Using warm water will speed up the rate at which the salt combines with the water and ensure that the salt dissolves.

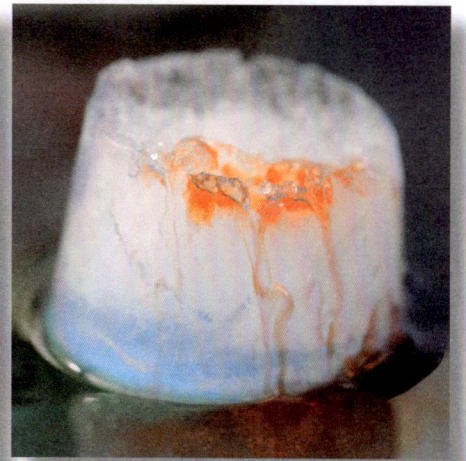

# Next level learning

Salt is an ionic compound. Investigate ionic compounds to determine what makes salt one.

Repeat the activity using different ratios of salt and water. Which concentration of salt melts the ice the quickest?

What happens if you use larger or smaller blocks of ice?

# Making curriculum links

| EYFS | Exploring colours, active learning, observation, communication, language, physical development, mathematics, imagination. |
|---|---|
| Primary | Working scientifically, working creatively, evaluating and testing ideas, colour, measuring, volume, mathematics. |
| Secondary | Working scientifically, colour, mathematics, ratio, solutions and saturation, problem solving, conceptual understanding, measurement, states of matter, ionic compounds, experimental skills and observation. |

# Activity 23
# Rainbow origami

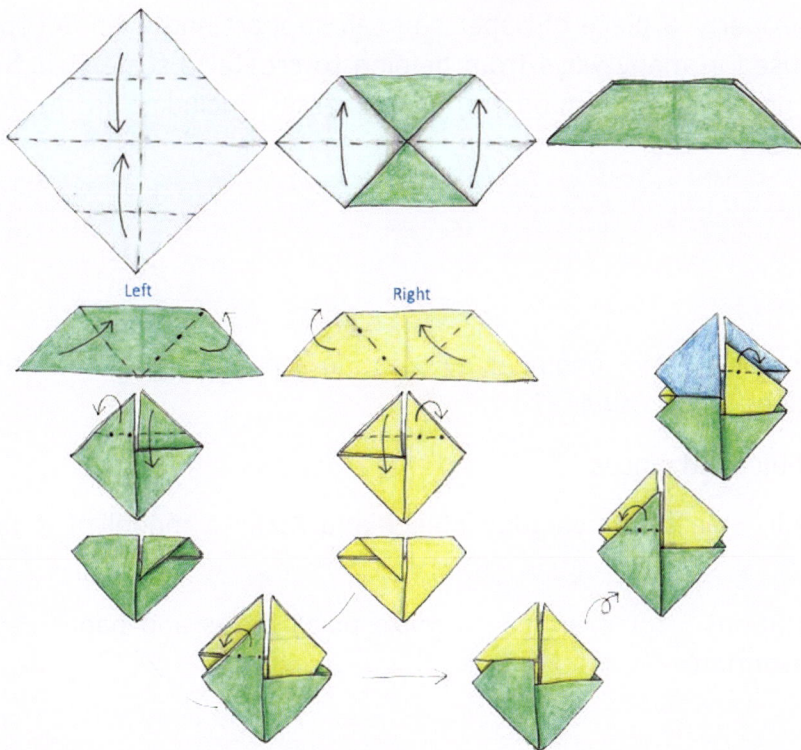

## The instructions

1. Using square pieces of paper we are going to repeat this process seven times.

2. Fold the first piece of paper in half.

3. Fold the bottom corners up to meet at the centre line.

4. Turn the paper over folding the top corners down to meet the centre line.

5. Your paper will now look like a triangle.

6. Turn this so the paper is pointing towards you.

---

1  As an alternative, use plain paper, which you'll need to cut down to size and colour in.

7. You will have created a small 'pocket' place your finger inside this.

8. Fold the paper in half to create two points that will look a bit like rabbit ears!

9. Repeat this for this colour of the rainbow.

10. It is now time to connect each colour of the rainbow, do this by slotting together the first two colours of the rainbow, the red and orange. The orange paper should be approximately half a centimetre from the red paper.

11. Turn the corners of the red paper into the 'pocket' of the orange paper on each side.

12. Repeat these steps with the yellow paper into the orange paper and so on until the rainbow is complete.

13. You will now be able to carefully pull the paper into the shape of a rainbow.[2]

# The science

Origami is the art of paper folding, which originated in the Far East. Paper can be considered weak and lacking substance but, if folded properly, a piece of paper can self-support and even become a load-bearing bridge. Origami can be used in many ways from helping to create to-scale structures, which can then be used for solving problems, to demonstrating processes, including in medicine, robotics, civil engineering and satellites.

# Next level learning

Are you able to follow in the footsteps of a NASA engineer by creating a new piece of technology for astronauts to take on future missions using origami?

Investigate how origami is used in medical advances.

Use origami as a problem-solving skill. Select an everyday object and make a model of it using origami.

Investigate origami's real-world applications – for example, to make pizza boxes and paper carrier bags. Can you come up with a new invention?

# Making curriculum links

| EYFS | Colour, active learning, observation, communication, language, physical development, mathematics, expressive arts. |
|---|---|
| Primary | Working scientifically, working creatively, evaluating and testing ideas, colour, mathematics, art and design. |
| Secondary | Working scientifically, mathematics, problem solving, conceptual understanding, measurement, observation, design and technology, engineering skills. |

2 See Dr Lizzie's YouTube Channel: https://www.youtube.com/playlist?list=UU4RXqmAFrGGKSRbO_t20E7Q

# Activity 24
# Sound rainbow

## Sound waves

### You will need

- 1 x metal spoon
- 1 x jug of water
- 7 x identical glasses of equal size and shape
- Food colouring (red, orange, yellow, green, blue, indigo, violet)

## The instructions

1. Arrange the empty glasses in a row. It's really important that they are of an equal size and shape.

2. Using a metal spoon, tap each one of the glasses. Record your observations. (They should all sound the same.)

3. Pour a different amount of water into each glass. To make it easier to see the different water levels, add food colouring to each glass. You don't strictly have to use the seven different colours for this experiment to work, but it will help when recording the results if you are able to differentiate by colour.

4. Using the same metal spoon, tap on each of the glasses again. Listen carefully and record your observations. The sounds will have changed.

# The science

Sound travels through a medium as a wave. When you tap on the glasses with the metal spoon it disturbs the particles in the glass, causing them to vibrate. A sound wave is created when the vibrations in the glass are transferred to the air surrounding the glass. When the glasses were empty, the vibrations and sounds were all the same, but adding different volumes of water caused the vibrations and sounds to change.

The glass with the largest volume of water will create the lowest pitch; the glass with the least amount of water will have the highest pitch. Therefore, you can change the pitch of the sound by altering the volume of water in the glass. Pitch is dependent on the frequency of the sound wave.

When you add more water to the glass, the pitch is low. The volume of water makes it more difficult for the particles to vibrate, which causes the vibrations to be slower and have a lower frequency. When a smaller volume of water is added to the glass, the pitch will be high because the particles vibrate more easily in air than in water, leading to faster vibrations with a higher frequency.

# Next level learning

Investigate pitch. Accurately measure out different volumes of water. What volume of water produces the highest pitch and what volume the lowest? How will you measure this?

Create your very own musical scale by varying the volume of water in each glass. A musical scale has eight notes, so you will require eight glasses. Have fun creating different tunes on your glasses. Is anyone able to guess the tune you are playing?

# Making curriculum links

| EYFS | Active learning, observation, communication, language, physical development, mathematics, music. |
|---|---|
| Primary | Working scientifically, working creatively, evaluating and testing ideas, mathematics, music. |
| Secondary | Working scientifically, mathematics, problem solving, measurement, experimental skills, observation, sound waves, particles. |

# Activity 25
# Spinning colour wheel

**Colour - Light**

## You will need

- 1 x small white paper plate
- 1 x pencil
- 1 x ruler
- 1 x protractor
- Scissors
- Blue tack
- Felt tip pens (red, orange, yellow, green, blue, indigo, violet)

**Be very careful when using scissors.**

## The instructions

1. Cut out the centre of the small white paper plate (i.e. cut off the fluted edge). As an alternative, if you do not have paper plates, create a template on white card by drawing around a small plate.

2. Using the ruler and pencil, draw a line across the centre to divide the circle into two halves.

3. You now need to make four quarters by drawing a perpendicular line through the circle. These quarters will be at right angles (90°). Using the protractor, draw lines at a 45° angle to turn the quarters into eight equal sections.

4. Get creative, colouring in each section a different colour of the rainbow.

5. When you've finished colouring, punch a hole in the centre of the circle where all the lines come together. Do this by placing a lump of blue tack on the back of the circle, and pushing the pencil through to create a hole. Please be careful when doing this. Remove the blue tack but leave the pencil in place.

6. Move the pencil between your hands, making the colour wheel spin. Observe what you see.

# The science

When light hits a coloured object most of it is absorbed and only one colour is reflected. Light is made up of all the colours of the rainbow. When you spin the wheel, it mixes all the different wavelengths of the coloured light together, creating white light. The faster you spin the wheel, the better the effect will be.

# Next level learning

Our eyes are able to perceive colour because of light-sensitive photoreceptors called rods and cones. Find out more about the eye and how we see. How does the brain communicate these ideas?

How would an artist use the spinning colour wheel? What could its uses be?

Create spinning colour wheels using different colour combinations. What happens when you spin the wheels at different speeds? What effects are you able to create with different colour combinations and speeds?

# Making curriculum links

| EYFS | Active learning, observation, communication, language, physical development, colour mixing. |
| --- | --- |
| Primary | Working scientifically, working creatively, evaluating and testing ideas, mathematics, light, colour. |
| Secondary | Working scientifically, mathematics, problem solving, measurement, experimental skills, observation, light, colour. |

# Activity 26
# Rainbow in a box

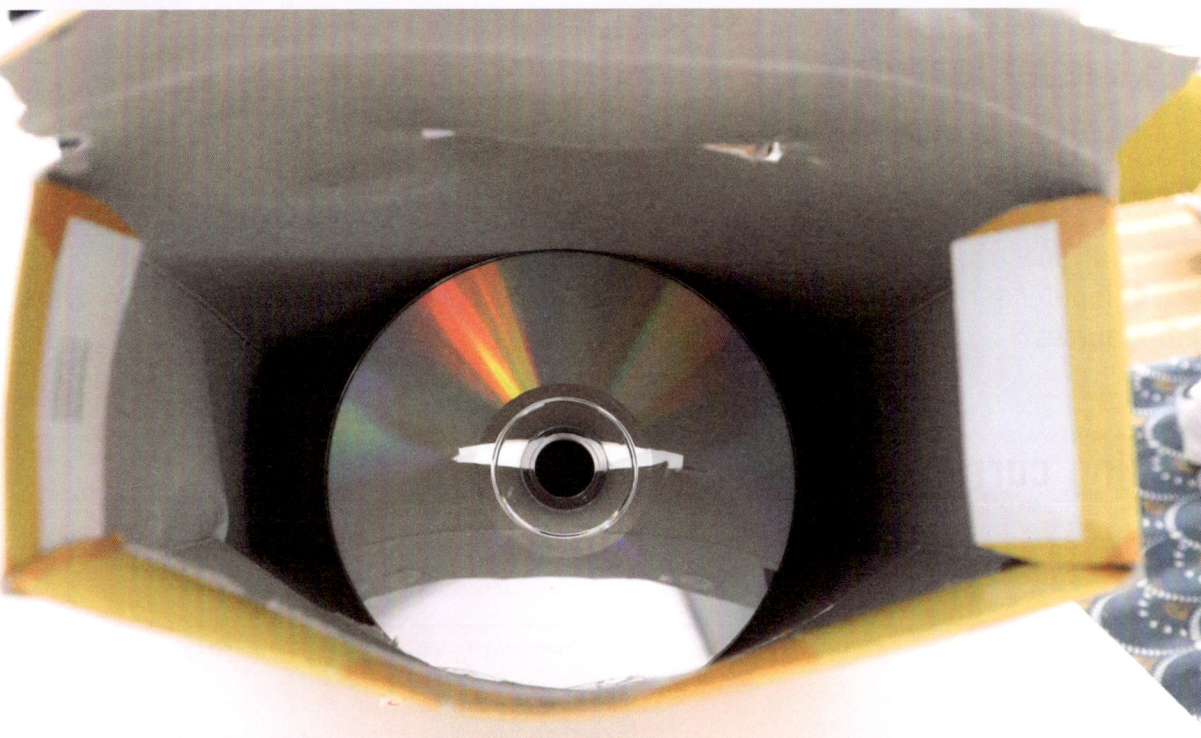

## You will need

- 1 x cardboard box
- 1 x old CD
- 1 x ruler
- Cardboard
- Scissors
- Sticky tape

## The instructions

1. Using a cardboard box, and using the photo (above) as a guide, start by creating two 2.5 cm cuts with the scissors on each side of the box at a 45° angle connecting these two cuts with a horizon cut along the edge of the box to create a holding place for the CD.

2. You now need to create a viewing window, this needs to be above the CD holding place approximately 2.5 cm from the top of the box, this area will allow you to see the spectra of light reflected from the CD.

3. Turn the box round. Now create a horizontal thin cut in the cardboard positioned just above the CD holder section on the opposite side to allow light to pass through onto the CD.

4. Place the CD in the section created for it.

5. Take your box outside on a sunny day pointing the top cut section up to the sky but making sure you never look directly at the sun.

6. Your rainbow will appear inside the box!

# The science

You have created your very own spectroscope. This is a piece of equipment used for producing and recording spectra for examination. What this means is it breaks down light from a single material into its component colours. Equipment like this allows scientists to discover and study the properties of light. The CD is a mirrored surface with information encoded in small grooves which are evenly spaced and diffract light. The light diffracts (spreads out) when it hits the surface of the CD, creating a rainbow as it passes through the narrow cuts in the cardboard box. Depending on the source of the light, some colours will appear darker or brighter than others.

# Next level learning

Space scientists use spectroscopy to study light from space. Investigate how spectroscopy is used in the study of stars, temperature, density and environments.

Test your spectroscope with other light sources – for example, a fluorescent light bulb, a TV screen or a computer screen. What do you notice? Do any colours appear lighter or darker with the differing light sources?

# Making curriculum links

| EYFS | Exploring colours, active learning, observation, communication, language, physical development, expressive arts. |
|---|---|
| Primary | Working scientifically, working creatively, evaluating and testing ideas, light, colour, expressive arts, design and technology. |
| Secondary | Working scientifically, mathematics, problem solving, measurement, experimental skills, observation, light, colour, space science, design and technology, engineering skills. |

# Activity 27
# Rainbow bread

## Chemical reactions – Enzymes

### You will need

- 1 x rolling pin
- 1 x oven
- 1 x wooden spoon
- 1 x loaf tin
- 1 x whisk
- 1 x cup of milk
- 1 x egg

- 1 x packet of active dry yeast
- 1 x small mixing bowl
- 1 x large mixing bowl
- 1.5 x teaspoons of unsalted butter (plus extra for greasing)
- 2 x teaspoons of salt
- 2.5 x teaspoons of white granulated sugar

- 3 x cups of all-purpose flour
- 5 x medium bowls
- Food colouring (red, yellow, green, blue, purple)
- Cling film
- Greaseproof paper

**Adult supervision while using the oven is essential.**

# The instructions

1. Start by greasing the five medium sized bowls.

2. Separate the egg yolk from the egg white.

3. Whisk together the egg yolk and the milk.

4. Add the flour, sugar, yeast, butter and salt to the large mixing bowl. Combine with the milk and egg mixture to make your dough.

5. Knead the dough for about ten minutes until the mixture is smooth and elastic.

6. Split the dough into five equal parts.

7. Take one part of the dough and add food colouring – ten drops will produce a deep colour. Continue to knead until the food colouring is evenly distributed. Place the dough into a medium greased bowl, covering the bowl with cling film. Repeat this process with each colour. Then leave the dough to rise for two hours.

8. Grease the loaf tin and line with greaseproof paper.

9. Check that the dough in each bowl has at least doubled in size.

10. Flour the rolling pin before rolling each coloured dough ball into a rectangle, making sure they fit in your tin. Add the rectangles of dough to the tin, arranging in rainbow colour order. Cover with cling film and leave for a further hour.

11. Preheat the oven to 190° Celsius.

12. Remove the cling film and place the loaf tin in the oven for 30 minutes. You'll know when the bread is cooked because a knife or skewer will come away clean when stuck in it.

13. Leave to cool before slicing to reveal your rainbow bread.

# The science

There is so much STEAM in this experiment. The yeast is full of small single-celled organisms that feed off the sugar. This process gives off carbon dioxide, explaining why the dough doubles in size – the carbon dioxide expands within the dough when the dough is kept warm. This stage of bread making is called proving. Storing the dough at too low or too high a temperature while it is proving inhibits this reaction. The ingredients change state as the yeast ferments and also as the bread is baked in the oven, causing the change from a soft dough to a set loaf.

# Next level learning

Investigate the proteins in the flour, how salt plays its part, the enzymes contained in the yeast plus those involved in digestion and how carbon dioxide helps the bread to rise. There is so much behind a humble loaf of bread!

Think about bread construction projects. What could you create from dough?

What would happen if you used different quantities of the ingredients? Experiment with using different amounts of flour, yeast, salt, milk, etc. Note that these results won't necessarily be edible.

# Making curriculum links

| EYFS | Active learning, observation, communication, language, physical development, colour mixing, mathematics. |
| --- | --- |
| Primary | Working scientifically, working creatively, colour, states of matter. |
| Secondary | Working scientifically, mathematics, problem solving, measurement, experimental skills, observation, colour, design and technology, cells, nutrition and digestion, cellular respiration, chemical reactions, energy, enzymes. |

# Activity 28
# Rainbow suncatchers

## Colour - Light

## You will need

- 1 x bowl
- 1 x paintbrush
- 1 x protective surface
- Tissue paper (red, orange, yellow, green, blue, indigo, violet)
- Card
- PVA glue
- String
- Sticky tape
- Plastic wallets
- Scissors

## The instructions

1. Cut the edges off of a plastic wallet so that you can open it up and lay it flat on a protective surface.

2. Pour PVA glue into a small bowl.

3. Tear the tissue paper into small pieces, creating piles of tissue paper in your different colours.

4. Create a rainbow template out of card. Glue this to one side of the plastic wallet.

5. Start to create your suncatcher by sticking the tissue paper to the plastic using a paintbrush and PVA glue. Build up the layers of colours within your rainbow template.

6. Fold the plastic wallet over your completed design and glue it into place. Leave to dry overnight. Once dry, carefully cut around the card. Add a loop of string to the top of the rainbow, securing in place with sticky tape to allow you to hang your creation in a window.

## The science

Your suncatcher is like a piece of stained glass. The suncatcher will be made of all different shapes, patterns, angles and dimensions. Clear glass permits more light to pass through it while coloured glass changes the wavelengths and diffuses the light. What colours produce the best reflection when angled in the sun? Which surfaces produce the best reflection and at what time of day and season?

# Next level learning

Research the process of how stained glass is made, investigating the links to metals and metal oxides and how stained glass reflects light.

Think about patterns, shapes and geometry. Make a suncatcher using different mathematical and random sizes, shapes, angles and dimensions.

Investigate other materials you could use to create suncatchers. Think about what materials to use as the 'glass' and different mediums to create the colour.

# Making curriculum links

| EYFS | Exploring colours, active learning, observation, communication, language, physical development, shape, expressive art and design. |
|---|---|
| Primary | Working creatively, colour, art and design, light, shape. |
| Secondary | Working scientifically, problem solving, observation, colour, design and technology. |

# Activity 29
# Rainbow crystals

## Crystals - Solutions

**Ask an adult to boil the kettle and take care when handling hot water.**

# The instructions

1. Place a skewer on top of each of the seven containers. Each skewer will need to be long enough to span the width of the container.

2. Cut seven lengths of string. They need to be long enough to tie around the skewers and reach the bottoms of the containers.

3. Take two bowls and add sugar to one and water to the other.

4. Dip each string in the water, then in the sugar. This will create a wick to attract your sugar crystals. Leave the wicks to dry overnight.

5. In a bowl, add four parts sugar to one part boiled water. Be extremely careful when handling hot water. Stir to dissolve the sugar.

6. Divide the sugar and water solution between your seven containers. Add a different rainbow colour to each one.

7. Add a sugar wick to each container.

8. Now be patient and watch as your rainbow crystals grow over seven to fourteen days.

9. Once you are happy with the crystal formation, take the wicks out and allow them to dry. Enjoy your rainbow of crystals.

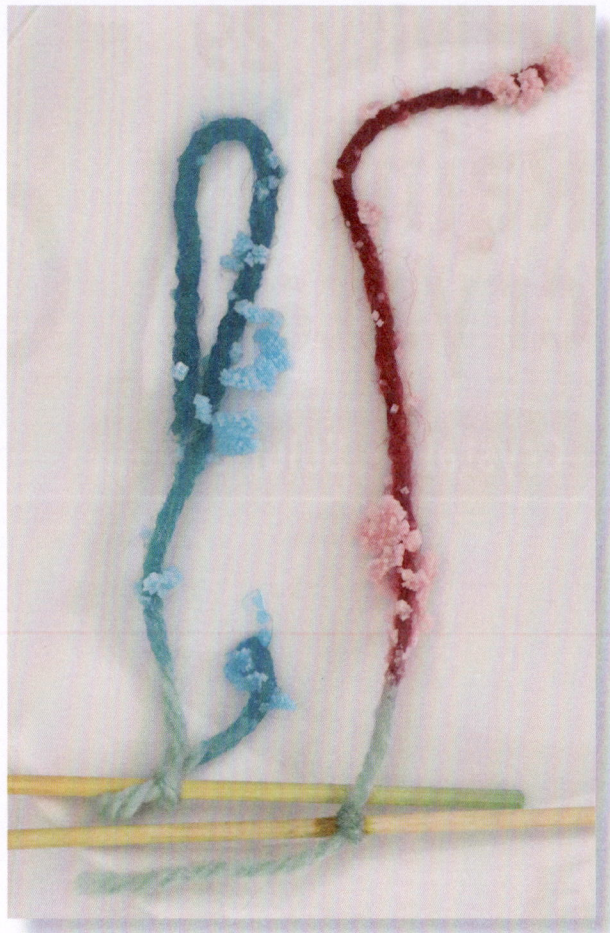

# The science

You have created a super saturated solution, meaning there is *more* sugar than can be dissolved in the water. The sugar molecules start to stick together, with the wick providing the sugar with somewhere to cling to, aiding the formation of the crystals.

# Next level learning

Are you able to create the ultimate sugar crystal? Investigate different sugar-to-water ratios. How are evaporation and precipitation involved in this process?

Create a crystal growing diary to record your observations on a daily basis.

Study the crystals you have grown. Take a close look at them. What are you able to see? Are you able to draw the crystals? Can you look at them under a microscope?

How are crystals formed in nature?

# Making curriculum links

| EYFS | Exploring colours, active learning, observation, communication, language, mathematics, shape. |
|------|-----------------------------------------------------------------------------------------------|
| Primary | Working creatively, colour, mathematics, working scientifically, observation, written skills. |
| Secondary | Working scientifically, mathematics, problem solving, measurement, observation, colour, solutions, ratios, matter, bonding, chemistry |

# Activity 30
# Rainbow in a bag

**Colour**

## You will need

- 1 x large zip-lock food bag
- 1 x protective surface
- Sticky tape
- Paint (red, yellow, blue)

## The instructions

1. Open the zip-lock food bag.

2. Add your paint to the inside of your bag. You want blobs of each colour in different areas.

3. Make sure the bag is securely fastened. In case of spillages, you could even put your bag on a protective surface or seal the bag with tape.

4. Now have fun moving the colours around inside the bag. Can you mix the colours to create a rainbow?

# The science

This colour mixing experiment is fun and sensory. Red, yellow and blue are primary colours and these mix to create secondary colours. However, the primary colours differ in painting and in physics. In art, red, yellow and blue are primary colours as the pigments are subtractive, but in light and physics, the primary colours are red, green and blue; they are additive (when you add all light colours, the result is white light).

# Next level learning

Research colour theories and the work of Newton. What can you find out about additive and subtractive colour mixing?

How many different colours are you able to make in the bag? What pictures are you able to create? Investigate paint ratios for the ultimate rainbow in a bag.

# Making curriculum links

| EYFS | Exploring colours, active learning, observation, communication, language, fine motor skills, sensory play. |
|------|---|
| Primary | Working creatively, colour, working scientifically, observation, motor skills. |
| Secondary | Working scientifically, problem solving, measurement, observation, colour, mixtures, subtractive and additive colours. |

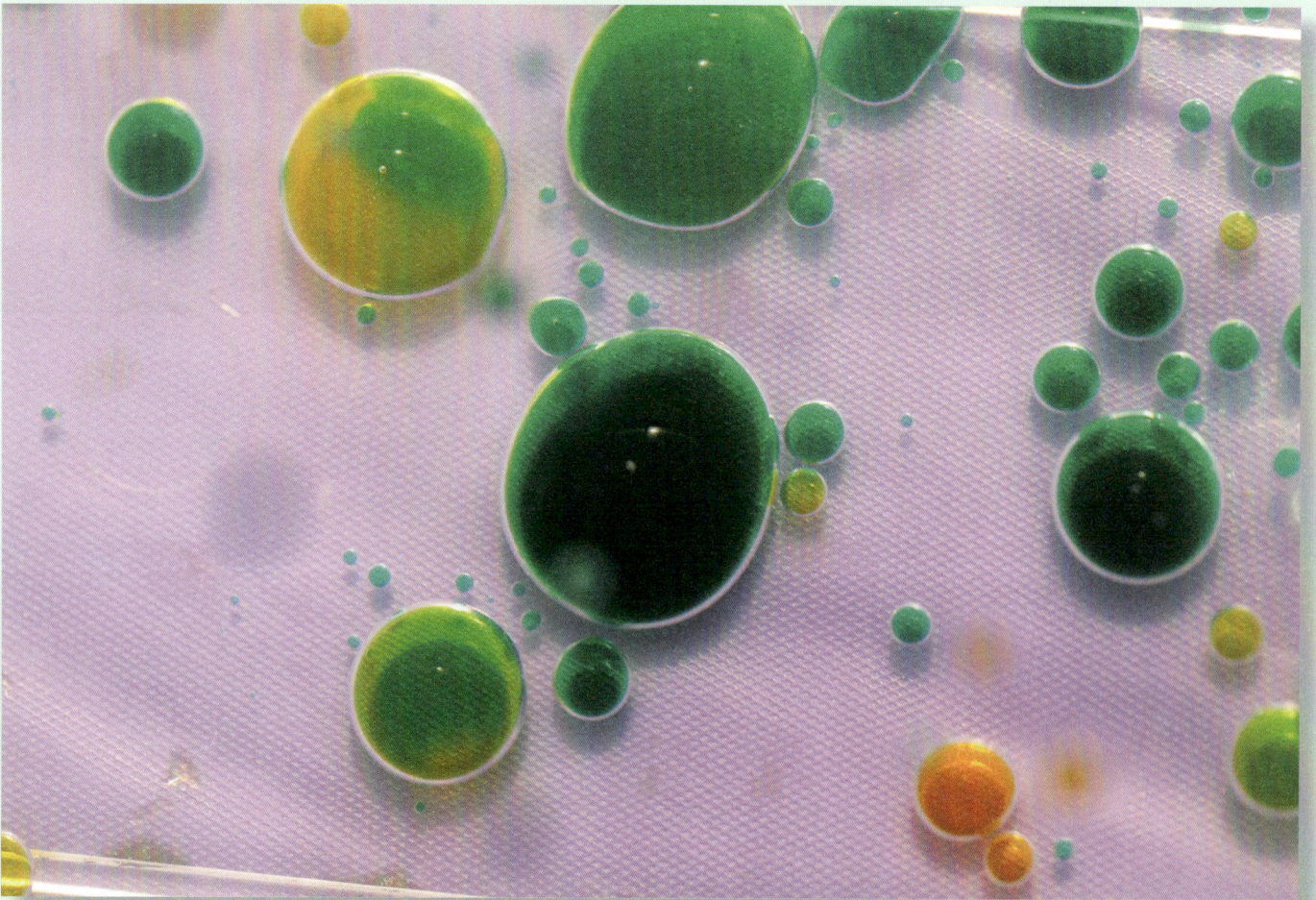

# Activity 31
# Oil and water rainbows

## Immiscible liquids

## You will need

- 1 x clear container
- 1 x spoon
- 7 x small containers
- 7 x pipettes
- Water
- Baby oil
- Food colouring (red, orange, yellow, green, blue, indigo, violet)

## The instructions

1.  Fill the small containers with water and add five drops of food colouring to each one (one colour in each container). Stir to combine the food colouring and water.

2.  Add a pipette to each of the containers. If you don't have enough pipettes, you could wash one out in between uses, but you want to avoid the colours mixing.

3.  Fill your clear container with oil. Baby oil works best because it is clear, but the experiment will work with other oils.

4.  Squeeze some of the red water into the pipette and drop it onto the oil in the container. Do not touch the surface of the oil with the pipette. Repeat with each of the colours.

5.  Observe what happens.

## The science

Oil and water do not mix. This is because they are immiscible. Water is a polar molecule, meaning it has one positively charged and one negatively charged end. This causes water molecules to stick together, as the positive end of a molecule is attracted to the negative end of another molecule. Oil is nonpolar, meaning it is evenly balanced. Because of this the oil molecules are not attracted to the water molecules, so they do not mix. Water is also denser than oil, causing the coloured water to sink through the oil layer.

# Next level learning

Investigate hydrogen bonds and how water is held together.

Complete a full investigation into what happens when you add different amounts of coloured water to the oil. What do you observe when large and small amounts are added? What happens if you stir the oil and water together?

# Making curriculum links

| EYFS | Active learning, observation, communication, language, physical development. |
|------|------------------------------------------------------------------------------|
| Primary | Working creatively, colour, working scientifically, observation, properties and changes to materials. |
| Secondary | Working scientifically, problem solving, measurement, observation, colour, mixtures, density, structure and properties of matter. |

# Activity 32

# Sweet wrapper coloured filters

## You will need

- Transparent sweet wrappers in different colours
- Scissors
- Cardboard tubes (e.g. from toilet or kitchen roll)
- Sticky tape
- Laminator (optional)
- Laminator pouches (optional)
- Hole punch (optional)
- String (optional)

# The instructions

1. If you have access to a laminator, flatten the sweet wrappers out and laminate them first. Cut out the different colour squares and punch a hole in one corner of each of the squares. Thread them together with string. You have created a colour wheel. View the world through the different colours. Investigate colour combinations by placing different colours on top of one another. Make a prediction before testing which secondary and tertiary colours will be made.

2. If you do not have access to a laminator, this is not a problem. Simply use the wrappers as light filters, holding them up to the light or placing them over an object to observe what colour it turns. Tape several different colours together to see what happens.

3. Create binoculars and telescopes by taping the sweet wrappers over the end of the cardboard tubes. To create a telescope, use one long tube. To create a pair of binoculars, use two shorter cardboard tubes taped together. You could add string so the binoculars can be worn around your neck, and have fun decorating them.

## The science

Certain wavelengths of colour are absorbed by the coloured filters, with other wavelengths transmitted, allowing the colour to be seen. Light is the source of colour. An example of this is a red apple. The apple absorbs all the colour wavelengths apart from red, which it reflects, making it appear red.

## Next level learning

What is the science behind colour? How do animals see and why is this?

Use the colour wheel to make secondary colours. Red and yellow make orange; yellow and blue make green; blue and red produce purple.

Discuss what your favourite colours are. How does the world look when you see it in different colours? Do different colours make objects appear darker? Brighter? More difficult to see?

Play a colour matching game. Are you able to find objects that match the colours of the sweet wrappers?

When are coloured filters used in the real world and why? Think in terms of photography and concerts. Create your own concert stage setup in a cardboard box complete with lighting and coloured filters.

# Making curriculum links

| EYFS | Active learning, observation, communication, language, colour mixing, understanding the world. |
|------|-----------------------------------------------------------------------------------------------|
| Primary | Working creatively, colour, working scientifically, observation, light. |
| Secondary | Working scientifically, problem solving, observation, colour, light, waves. |

# Activity 33
# Rainbow oobleck

## Non-Newtonian fluids

### You will need

- 1 x cup of water
- 1 x mixing bowl
- 1 x spoon
- 2 x cups of cornstarch
- Food colouring
- Cling film (optional)
- Speaker (optional)
- Music player (e.g. smartphone) (optional)

**Do not allow the ooblek to come in direct contact with any part of the electronics.**

## The instructions

1. Add two cups of cornstarch to a mixing bowl.

2. Mix a couple of drops of food colouring into one cup of water.

3. Add the coloured water to the mixing bowl and stir to combine with the cornstarch.

4. If you want to make rainbow oobleck, repeat steps 1–3 for each different colour. Make each colour in separate batches then pour them together.

5. To make your oobleck dance, connect the speaker to your smartphone. Test the audio – around 40Hz usually works well.

6. Cover the speaker with cling film, and place the oobleck onto the cling film.

7. Play a low frequency test tone. The vibrations of the speaker will cause the oobleck to move in a 'dance'.

# The science

Oobleck is a non-Newtonian fluid. This is a liquid that changes viscosity dependent on pressure. It is neither a solid nor a liquid, but both. A non-Newtonian fluid does not follow Newton's law of viscosity, moving like a liquid but also able to be held and broken like a solid.

# Next level learning

Observe how the oobleck behaves. You may wish to see how it feels in your hands or even under your feet! Can you try to paint with it? Will it pour? Watch as it dribbles through the holes in the bottom of a used fruit punnet or a colander.

Investigate sound and how we hear combined with frequency. Play different test tones and observe how it changes the 'dance' of the oobleck.

Investigate other non-Newtonian fluids like ketchup and honey.

# Making curriculum links

| EYFS | Active learning, observation, communication, language, colour mixing, understanding the world, sensory play. |
|---|---|
| Primary | Working creatively, colour, working scientifically, observation, sound, matter. |
| Secondary | Working scientifically, problem solving, observation, colour, waves, sound, viscosity, states of matter. |

# Activity 34
# Kaleidoscope

## Colour - Light - Pattern

### You will need

- 1 x plastic container (a plastic cup works well)
- 1 x ruler
- 2 x cardboard tubes
- Tin foil or shimmery paper
- Glue
- Tissue paper
- Sequins
- Sticky tape
- Mirrored card
- Scissors

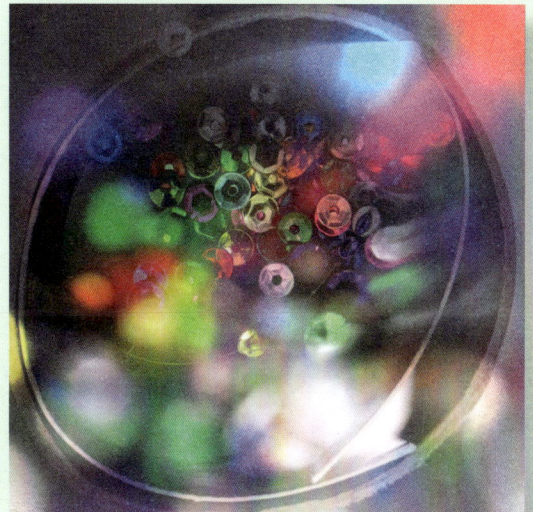

## The instructions

1. Line a cardboard tube with shimmery paper or tin foil.

2. Get as creative as you like on the outside of the cardboard tube: draw, paint, colour or cover in paper.

3. Form a prism with your mirrored card by cutting three stripes of the mirrored card, sticking them together with sticky tape along the long edges making sure the shiny side is facing inwards. You will need to make sure this fits inside your cardboard tube. If using a kitchen roll tube with the size 20 cm x 4.5 cm, your mirrored card prism will work if cut to 19 cm x 4.3 cm. Fit the mirrored card prism into the cardboard tube leaving an area of 1 cm from the end of the tube.

4. Using the second cardboard tube, cut a 2 cm section. This will form a cap on the end of the first tube.

5. Using the small tube as a template, cut two circles from the plastic container.

6. Secure one of the plastic circles to the end of the small tube with sticky tape.

7. Fill this tube with sequins.

8. Using the second plastic circle, secure this inside the small tube to keep the sequins from escaping!

9. Connect the small tube to the large tube resting at the mirrored card prism.

10. Turn the section at the end to create your kaleidoscope.

# The science

A kaleidoscope is an optical instrument that works by reflecting light between reflective surfaces in a confined space. The reflective surfaces are tilted at each other and light and mirrors are used to reflect objects creating repeating patterns. The more reflective surfaces there are inside the kaleidoscope, the more the patterns change.

# Next level learning

Calculate the best angles to use in your kaleidoscope to make the most patterns.

Investigate what a kaleidoscope is used for in real-world situations.

Draw the patterns created by your kaleidoscope and turn this into a piece of fashion.

# Making curriculum links

| EYFS | Active learning, observation, communication, language, pattern, understanding the world, expressive art and design, sensory play. |
|------|---------------------------------------------------------------------------------------------------------------------------------|
| Primary | Working creatively, colour, working scientifically, observation, light, pattern, mathematics, art and design. |
| Secondary | Working scientifically, problem solving, observation, colour, light, angles, problem solving, art and design. |

# Activity 35
# Rainbow mandala

**Colours in nature**

**You will need**

- Natural materials (e.g. sticks, grass, stones, flowers, leaves)

# The instructions

1. You would be able to create a mandala with any objects, but it would be fantastic to get outside and create one from nature. Start by collecting all of your materials. Try to find objects that are different colours of the rainbow. Look for anything you are able to safely find on the ground and ask an adult before picking anything that is living (flowers, leaves, etc.).

2. Locate an open surface - for example, a table, playground or area of grass.

3. Now is the time to get really creative by laying out your objects to create the full circle of a rainbow.

# The science

The shape of a circle symbolises how nature does not begin or end but is always connected - the same as a rainbow. Rainbows are actually full circles. On the ground you will only see the light reflected by raindrops on the horizon. You will never reach the end of a rainbow because raindrops act like little prisms. The raindrops split light up into bands of colour. Colours you see in a rainbow come from millions of raindrops that are sitting at different angles in the sky, splitting the sunlight into colours for your eyes to see. As you move toward the rainbow, the angles change. In order for the angles to work out, the raindrops have to be a certain distance from your eyes. No matter how you move, the rainbow will always be the same distance away from you, resulting in you never reaching the end of the rainbow.

# Next level learning

Find out the proper name of a circular rainbow. Why is a rainbow curved and when would it be possible to view a full circular rainbow?

Investigate the science behind the art of a mandala and find other patterns in nature.

What patterns are you able to create? Try starting in the centre and really think about the symmetry of your pattern. Are you able to create a mandala with one side mirroring the other?

# Making curriculum links

| EYFS | Exploring colours, active learning, counting, observation, communication, language, pattern, understanding the world, expressive art and design. |
|---|---|
| Primary | Working creatively, colour, working scientifically, observation, pattern, mathematics, art and design. |
| Secondary | Working scientifically, problem solving, observation, colour, shape, art and design. |

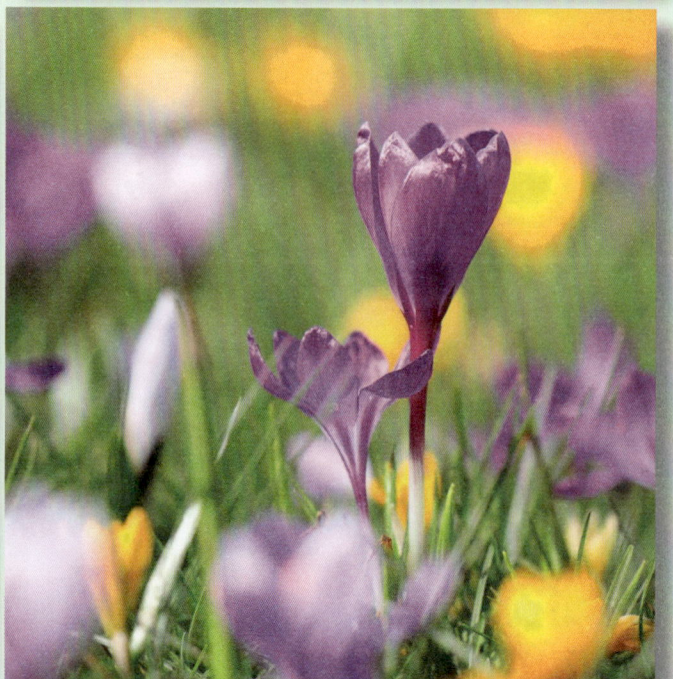

# Activity 36
# Secret messages

## You will need

- 1 x red pen
- 1 x blue pen
- White paper
- Red and blue transparent sweet wrappers (or coloured filters)

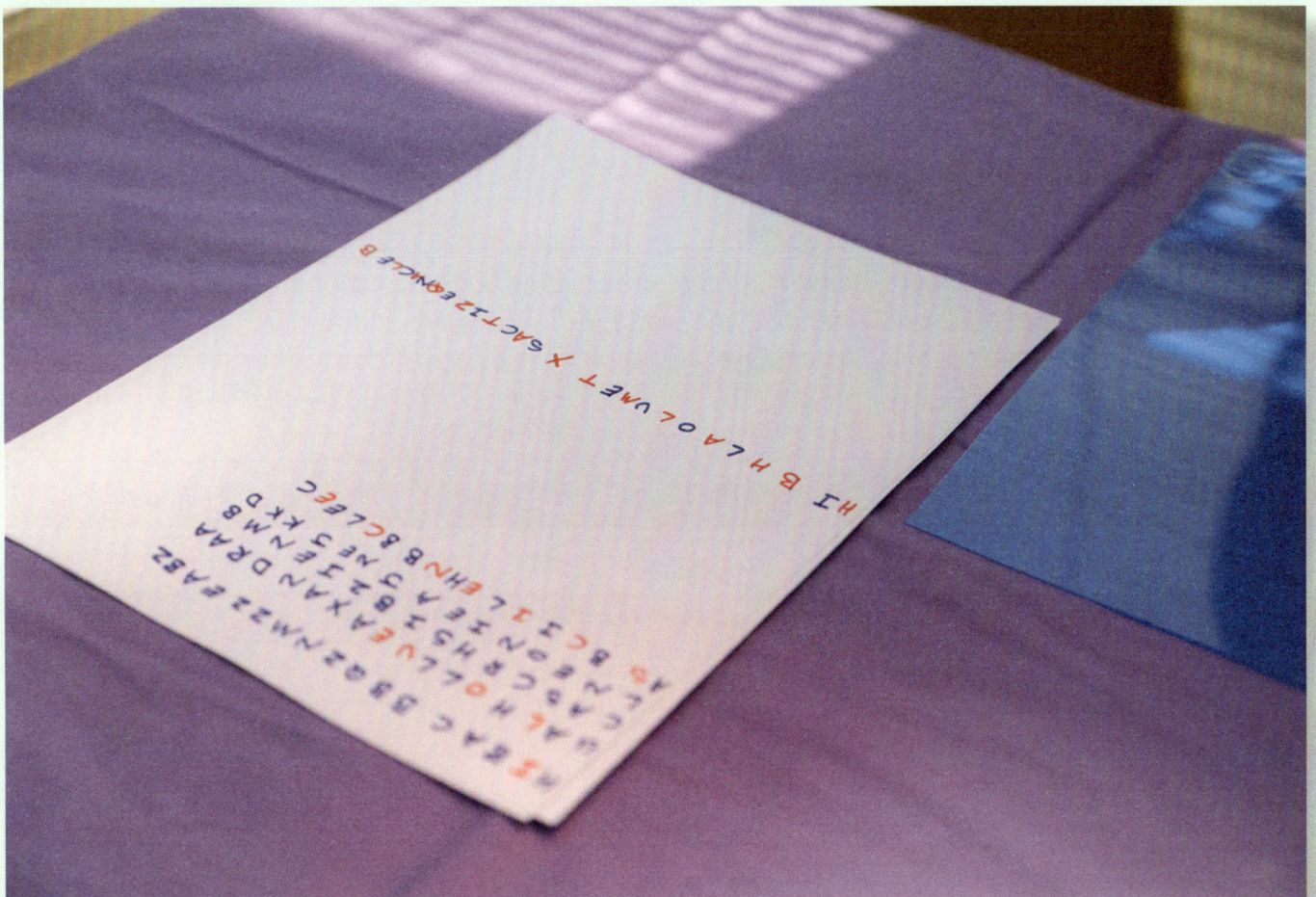

# The instructions

1. On your sheet of white paper write out your secret message using your blue pen, leaving a space between each letter.

2. Fill in the spaces using your red pen, creating another secret message.

3. Put your blue sweet wrapper over the writing to reveal the secret message in red.

4. Put the red sweet wrapper over the writing to reveal the secret message in blue.

# The science

The coloured ink seems to disappear when viewed under the same colour of sweet wrapper as that wavelength of light is absorbed. As you view the writing on white paper under the red sweet wrapper, the red writing can no longer be seen! As you place the blue sweet wrapper over the writing, you are only able to see the message written in red, not blue, therefore revealing the secret message.

# Next level learning

Create your own secret code and see if anyone is able to decipher it. Investigate code breakers and their importance in history.

Repeat the activity with different colour sweet wrappers and different colour pens. You'll just need to find a pen that matches the colour of your sweet wrapper and away you go! Which colours were the most difficult to read?

# Making curriculum links

| EYFS | Exploring colours, active learning, observation, communication, language, pattern, writing skills, understanding the world, expressive art and design. |
|---|---|
| Primary | Working creatively, colour, working scientifically, observation, pattern, mathematics, art and design. |
| Secondary | Working scientifically, problem solving, observation, colour, shape, art and design. |

H BAC BBQZNMZZEABZ
UA H LL AXANDRAA
CASCRHSIBZIENMB
LNEONIEAJNEJKKD
A B I L H BB LE C
I LOVE SCIENCE

# Activity 37
# Rainbow diffusion

**Diffusion**

# The instructions

1. Sort your sweets into groups dependent upon colour.

2. Place your sweets around the inner edge of the plate, alternating the colours.

3. Carefully pour water from the jug into the centre of the plate.

4. Observe what takes place.

# The science

Skittles, and similar sweets, are coated in sugar and food colouring. When this coating comes into contact with water, it causes it to dissolve. It then spreads through the water via a process called diffusion. Diffusion is the movement of a substance from an area of high concentration to an area of low concentration until equilibrium is reached. The water takes on the colour of the sweets, creating a rainbow.

# Next level learning

In which states of matter does diffusion take place and why? Investigate and explain why diffusion is a very important process in living organisms.

Time how long it takes for the different colours to reach the centre of the plate. Do all the colours behave the same, timing wise? How are you able to speed up the process of diffusion? Investigate using cold and warm water, recording your results and writing a conclusion.

# Making curriculum links

| EYFS | Exploring colours, active learning, counting, observation, communication, language, pattern, understanding the world, expressive art and design. |
|------|-------------------------------------------------------------------------------------------------------------------------------------------------|
| Primary | Working creatively, colour, working scientifically, observation, pattern, art and design. |
| Secondary | Working scientifically, problem solving, observation, colour, shape, art and design. |

# Activity 38
# Rainbow slime

**Polymers**

Avoid slime making activities if pregnant.
The slime activator contains only 0.25% borax decahydrate, far below the 4.5% threshold that poses any risk.

# The instructions

1. Add three-quarters of a cup of clear glue to your bowl. Mix in half a teaspoon of baking soda.

2. Add your contact lens solution one teaspoon at a time, mixing each time a teaspoon full is added. You are aiming to create a mixture that has the consistency of ketchup.

3. Add the food colouring (five to ten drops should be enough) and mix. This can get messy, so wear gloves and old clothes, or an apron, and work on a protective surface.

4. Knead and mix thoroughly until your slime begins to form. Continue to knead and stretch the slime. Over time it will become less sticky.

5. If you want to create a rainbow of slime, you will need to repeat steps 1-4 for each colour.

# The science

Adding the contact lens solution to the glue forms a viscous substance that can be shaped and stretched. A bond is created between the borate ions and the glue molecules, resulting in the molecules no longer having the ability to easily slide past each other. This reaction creates the slime substance.

# Next level learning

Slime is a polymer. Investigate polymers and how they are widely used.

Have a competition to see who is able to make the stretchiest slime. How could you alter the method to improve the stretchiness?

# Making curriculum links

| EYFS | Exploring colours, active learning, counting, observation, communication, language, understanding the world, expressive art and design. |
| --- | --- |
| Primary | Working creatively, colour, working scientifically, observation, pattern, matter, art and design, chemical changes. |
| Secondary | Working scientifically, problem solving, observation, colour, shape, mathematics, polymers, chemical reactions, structure of matter. |

# Activity 39
# Rainbow bouncing eggs

**Chemical reactions**

## You will need

- 1 x jar
- 1 x egg
- 1 x spoon
- 1 x protective surface
- White vinegar
- Food colouring

## The instructions

1. Carefully place the egg into the jar.

2. Fill the jar with white vinegar until the egg is fully submerged. Add ten drops of food colouring, stirring carefully until it is evenly distributed.

3. Leave the egg in the jar for two to three days. During this time make any observations you can – for example, are there any changes in the egg? Has anything happened to the vinegar? Continue with this process until the egg looks translucent (meaning it allows the light to pass through it).

4.  Taking care, remove the egg from the jar and rinse it under the cold tap.

5.  As you are rinsing the egg, gently rub it until the shell (the outer layer) is removed. This will look like a white film and your egg will appear translucent. Record your observations again.

6.  Working on a protective surface, lift your egg no more than 5 cm in the air. Let your egg go and watch it bounce! How high are you able to lift the egg before it splats on impact?

# The science

So, just how did your egg become bouncy?! This was a result of a chemical reaction. The reaction took place between the vinegar and the eggshell. The eggshell is made of calcium carbonate and the vinegar is an acid. The calcium carbonate reacts with the vinegar. You are able to see that a reaction is taking place because bubbles form around the egg as the vinegar is added. These bubbles are carbon dioxide gas, caused by the reaction between the acid and the carbonate. Once the chemical reaction results in dissolving the shell, all that remains to cover the egg is a thin membrane. The membrane of a chicken egg is semipermeable, so the vinegar is able to cross it via the process of osmosis. The vinegar toughens up the membrane making it bouncy!

# Next level learning

Why is the yolk still yellow in your bouncing egg?

Experiment with colour by repeating the activity using all the different colours of the rainbow.

Keep a diary recording your observations about how the eggs are changing in the vinegar.

Add eggs to different solutions (e.g. sugar, salt, etc.) to see if you achieve the same outcome.

# Making curriculum links

| EYFS | Exploring colours, active learning, counting, observation, communication, language, understanding the world. |
|------|--------------------------------------------------------------------------------------------------------------|
| Primary | Working creatively, colour, working scientifically, observation, living things. |
| Secondary | Working scientifically, problem solving, observation, colour, mathematics, chemical reactions, osmosis. |

# Activity 40
# Rainbow ice orbs

**States of matter**

## The instructions

### You will need

- 1 x jug of water
- 1 x freezer
- 7 x balloons
- Food colouring (red, orange, yellow, green, blue, indigo, violet)
- Scissors

1. Squeeze ten drops of food colouring into a balloon.

2. Fill the balloon with water, making sure it is securely tied at the top. Shake it to make sure the colour is distributed.

3. Repeat steps 1-2 for each colour of the rainbow.

4. Add the balloons to the freezer. If it is winter, you could leave them outside to freeze.

5. Once frozen, carefully cut off the balloon to reveal your rainbow of ice orbs.

6. Now it is time to get creative. What will you make with yours? A caterpillar? A tower? Could you hang them in a tree, or display them in your garden or in the school grounds?

# The science

When water freezes it changes state from a liquid to a solid. Liquid water molecules are in constant motion. As the liquid water changes state to solid ice, the molecules slow down, lining up in a regular formation.

# Next level learning

Have fun creating ice structures.

Investigate states of matter as the water turns from a liquid to a solid, then back to a liquid again.

Create different size ice orbs using different volumes of water. Which takes the longest time to melt? Are you able to speed up the melting process?

# Making curriculum links

| EYFS | Exploring colours, active learning, counting, observation, communication, understanding the world. |
|------|---------------------------------------------------------------------------------------------------|
| Primary | Working creatively, colour, working scientifically, observation, states of matter, materials. |
| Secondary | Working scientifically, problem solving, observation, colour, states of matter, molecular structure. |

# Conclusion

## STEAM subjects are for everyone

The aim of this book is to inspire children and young people to discover, interact with, enjoy and take STEAM subjects further, developing a lifelong love of these topics. To be able to play a small part in this journey is extremely exciting and fulfilling. With a skills shortage noted in these areas, now is the time to engage young people to fulfil these roles and take on STEAM-based careers, to the benefit of everyone in the future.[1] Who knows who might follow in the footsteps of Tim Peake, Rosalind Franklin or David Attenborough? It's exciting to think of the discoveries that will be made in years to come by new generations of creative STEAM experts.

We've explored how to bring a vibrant, rainbow-inspired STEAM curriculum to life in a way that engages and empowers learners of all backgrounds and breaks down barriers to make these subjects more accessible. By weaving the colours of the rainbow throughout your STEAM curriculum, you can spark curiosity, cultivate creativity, develop essential life skills and nurture the next generation of innovative thinkers while bringing a sense of achievement and joy, cultivating a truly impactful approach to learning.

As you conclude this journey, remember that your vibrant approach is not just the start – it's a gateway to a world of endless possibilities.

Get ready to make your rainbow shine and transform the way learners experience STEAM learning.

---

1   See, for example, https://www.theiet.org/media/8186/addressing-the-stem-skill-s-shortage-challenge-report.pdf.

# About the author

**Leonie Briggs** is a science teacher, STEAM lead, STEM Ambassador, CREST Assessor and Director of Amazelab. With a varied background in STEM – ranging from veterinary and general practice to orthopaedics – she eventually discovered her passion for education and has held various roles as a primary, secondary, post 16 and alternative provision teacher specialising in science and chemistry.

Leonie's dedication has won her multiple accolades, including 'Outstanding New STEM Ambassador' (STEM Inspiration Awards, 2022), nominations for the Global Teacher Prize (2021) and the National Teaching Awards (2022), recognition as one of the UK's Top 100 Female Entrepreneurs (2025) and a Green Growth Awards finalist (2025).

Under her leadership, Amazelab has won UK Enterprise Awards for STEAM Education (2023 & 2024), Start-Up Business of the Year (2022) and STEAM Education Platform of the Year (2025).

Useful videos are available on the Amazelab YouTube channel: https://www.youtube.com/channel/UCPJVGxCQUA6mYsXy9XecqzQ/videos

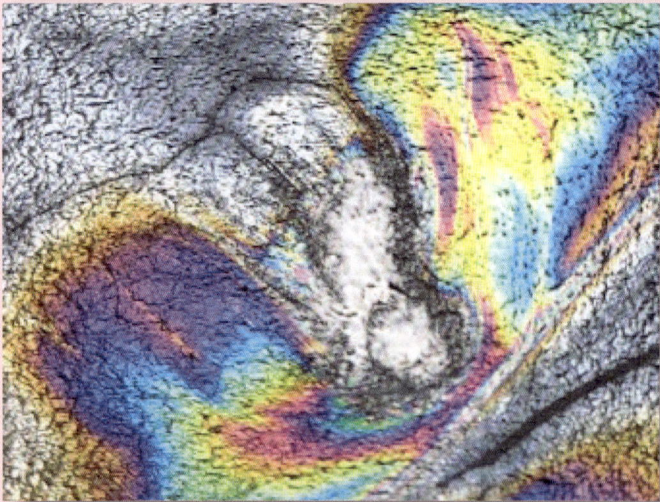